HIGHWAY TO HEAVEN SERIES
EDWARD A. FITZPATRICK, *Editor*
Institute of Catechetical Research, Marquette University

THE LIFE OF THE SOUL

BOOK OF THE HOLY CHILD (Grade One)

LIFE OF MY SAVIOR (Grade Two)

LIFE OF THE SOUL (Grade Three)

BEFORE CHRIST CAME (Grade Four)

THE VINE AND THE BRANCHES (Grade Five)

THE MISSAL (Grade Six)

HIGHWAY TO GOD (Grades Seven and Eight)

Accompanying this Series is the RELIGION IN LIFE CURRICULUM for grades one to six and PRACTICAL PROBLEMS IN RELIGION for grades seven and eight.

HIGHWAY TO HEAVEN SERIES III

The Life of the Soul

Prepared (*in co-operation with a group of priests
and sisters teaching in elementary schools*)
IN THE CATECHETICAL INSTITUTE OF
MARQUETTE UNIVERSITY
GEORGE H. MAHOWALD, S.J., PH.D., *Chairman*
RAPHAEL N. HAMILTON, S.J., PH.D.
GERARD SMITH, S.J., M.A.

By

EDWARD A. FITZPATRICK, PH.D.
Director of the Catechetical Institute

INCLUDING QUESTIONS FROM THE
BALTIMORE CATECHISM

ST. AUGUSTINE ACADEMY PRESS
HOMER GLEN, ILLINOIS

Nihil obstat:
  H. B. RIES,
      Censor librorum

Imprimatur:
  ✠ SAMUEL ALPHONSUS STRITCH,
      Archiepiscopus Milwaukiensis

May 6, 1932

The author gladly makes the following acknowledgments for permission to use the poems listed: To his Eminence William Cardinal O'Connell, for "O Sacred Cross" (p. 73); to the America Press, for Father Leonard Feeney, S.J., "The Way of the Cross" (p. 73); to Father E. F. Garesché, S.J., for "God's Home" (p. 99); to The Macmillan Company for the three poems from Mary Dixon Thayer's *A Child on His Knees* — "Different Ways" (p. 41), "After Communion" (p. 113), and "The Very Time" (p. 120).

This book was originally published in 1933 by The Bruce Publishing Company.
This edition reprinted in 2017 by St. Augustine Academy Press
based on the 1935 second printing.

Softcover ISBN: 978-1-64051-026-5
Hardcover ISBN: 978-1-64051-027-2

A LETTER TO YOU

My dear Little Reader:

This book tells you about your soul — the most important part of you. It tells you that your soul has a life just as your body has life. It tells how you can nourish this life of the soul with the sacraments which Christ Himself established just for that purpose. It makes clear how great the Roman Catholic Church is, which also was established by Christ Himself. You are a member of that Church. From it you receive the sacraments established by Christ to nourish and strengthen or restore the life of your soul.

Love your soul. It is God's gift to you. Take care of it. Keep from temptation and sin.

Love your soul. Love God the Father. Love God the Son. Love God the Holy Ghost. Love the Blessed Trinity. Seek the help in prayer of Mary, the Mother of God.

Keep in the Highway to Heaven. Stay on the road. Keep your end in view. Love your soul. Love God. Love His Church.

May this book help you to do these things. May it help your love of God and of your neighbor to abound more and more in knowledge as you learn about your holy religion.

Very sincerely yours,

Edward A. Fitzpatrick.

[5]

PART ONE

I. The Creation

1. The Body and Soul of Man

Man is composed of a body and soul.

I am a body and soul.

My soul tells my body what to do.

It says to the hand "take the book" and it does it.

It says to the legs "run," and they do it.

It says to the ears "listen," and they do it.

It says to the eyes "read," and they do it.

It says to the mouth "speak," and it does it.

The body obeys the soul.

The body must be kept in good health to obey the soul well.

The soul may tell the body to do good things or bad things.

It is the soul that is good or bad.

The body obeys the soul.

God wants my body to help my soul get to Heaven.

The soul is more important than the body.

The soul is more important than all the world.

I must love my soul more than my body.

We shall learn about the soul in this book.

We shall learn about the life of the soul.

We shall learn how we can keep it alive.

"In the beginning God created heaven, and earth"
(Gen. i. 1).

We shall learn how God created the soul of man.

We shall learn how we can make it more beautiful with God's help.

We shall learn how we can keep it beautiful until it returns to God.

Let us begin by learning how God created man, and the soul of man.

Of what is man composed?

What does the soul tell the hands? What do they do?

What does the soul tell the legs? What do they do?

What does the soul tell the ears? What do they do?

What does the soul tell the eyes? What do they do?

What does the soul tell the mouth? What does it do?

The body obeys the . . . .

Soul and . . . . must work together.

Is the soul always good?

God wants body and soul to work together in order to go to . . . .

Which is more important, soul or body? Why?

What are we going to learn in this book?

2. The Creation of Man

How God made Adam, the first man, we are told in the first book of the Bible.

He had made or created cattle.

He made things that creep on the earth.

He made beasts.

He made living things of all kinds.

He made all things.

And God saw that it was good.

God then said, "Let Us make man."

"Let Us make man to Our image and likeness."

And God did then create or make man in the image of God.

God made man.

It is the soul of man that is like God.

God gave man power over the fishes of the sea.

He gave man power over the fowls of the air.

He gave man power over the beasts.

He gave man power over every creeping thing upon the earth.

He gave man power over all the earth.

He made man and He made woman.

And God blessed the man and the woman.

He told them they would have children and fill the earth.

He told them to rule over it.

He told them to rule over the fishes of the sea.

He told them to rule over the fowls of the air.

He told them to rule over all the living creatures that
move on the earth.

And God saw that what He had made was good.

God created . . . .

God created all . . . .

God made man to His . . . . and . . . .

God made man and . . . .

God gave man power over all . . . .

God told man to rule over all . . . .

What book tells us these things?

Father in Heaven, We Thank Thee

For flowers that bloom about our feet,
For tender grass so fresh, so sweet,
For song of bird and hum of bee,
For all things fair we hear or see,
For blue of stream and blue of sky,
For pleasant shade of branches high,
For fragrant air and cooling breeze,
For beauty of the blooming trees,

For mother-love and father-care,
For brothers strong and sisters fair,
For love at home and here each day,
For guidance lest we go astray,
For this new morning with its light,
For rest and shelter of the night,
For health and food, for love and friends,
For ev'rything Thy goodness sends,
  Father in heaven, we thank Thee.
      — *Anonymous*

3. The Living Soul of Man

I shall tell you more about the first human soul.
God made it.
God took first the slime of the earth.
He formed man from it.
He breathed into his face the breath of life.
Man became a living soul.
Man is made of the slime of the earth and the breath
   of God.
He has a body.
He has a living soul.
Man is composed of body and soul.
God created him.
God created man in the image and likeness of Himself.
This likeness is in the soul.
God is a spirit.
My soul is a spirit.

God made . . . .
God made man's . . . .
God made man's . . . .
Man is composed of . . . . and . . . .
Man's soul is like . . . .
Man has a living . . . .
. . . . is a spirit.
My . . . . is a spirit.

4. God and the Soul

God lived before the mountains were made.

God lived before the sun and the moon and the stars were made.

God lived before the earth and the sky were made.

God always lived or existed.

God had no beginning.

Everything else had a beginning.

Everything began when God created it.

God has no end.

Everything God created on earth has an end, but the human soul.

That is the way God created the soul. It has a beginning, but it has no end.

God is eternal. He has no beginning and He has no end. He always was and He always will be. He lives forever.

God is a pure spirit. He has no body. He has no human sickness or ills. He is perfect in every way.

God is a spirit infinitely perfect.

We know, too, He is Love. We know He loves us. We shall learn in this book how great is His love for you and for me, for all men and women, and for all boys and girls. God is Love. Love God.

Did anything live before God?

God lived before the . . . .

God lived before the . . . . , the moon, and the . . . . were made.

God had no ....
God has no ....
The soul has a ....
The soul has no ....
I love ....
.... loves me.
.... is a spirit.
God is a pure ....
God is a spirit perfect in .... way.
God is a spirit infinitely ....

5. God Made Me

God made all things.
God made Adam.
God made all men.
God made me.
God made you.
God loves me. That is why I am here.
God made me to love Him. I love God.
God made my neighbor, too.
My love of my neighbor is service to God.
We should all love one another, because God made all
   of us. We are all His creatures.
He is the Father of all of us.
We are all children of God.
He is our Heavenly Father.
He made me to know Him.
He made me to love Him.
He made me to serve Him in this world.
He wants me to be happy with Him forever in Heaven.

God made me to . . . . Him.
God made me to . . . . Him.
God made me to . . . . Him.
. . . . love God.
. . . . love my neighbor, because God made him too.
. . . . love all God's creatures.
God wants me to be happy with Him in . . . .

6. God, the Father

God made the heavens and the earth.

He made you and He made me. He knows what goes on in our minds, and in our hearts. He knows what we think and what we feel. He knows our secret thoughts. We are His creatures. He is our Creator.

He made all things.

He is the Creator of Heaven and of earth and of all things.

He is our Father as we learned from Christ to call Him.

He is God, the Father.

He is Almighty.

He is the Creator of Heaven and earth and of all things.

I believe in God, the Father Almighty, Creator of Heaven and earth and of all things.

God made . . . . and . . . . God made all . . . .
Who made you? Who made me?
We are His . . . . is our Father.
Who taught us to call God our Father?
. . . . believe in God, the Father Almighty.
. . . . believe in God, the Creator of Heaven, and earth and of all things.

OUR Father Who art in heaven, hallowed be Thy name; Thy kingdom come; Thy will be done on earth as it is in heaven. Give us this day our daily bread; and forgive us our trespasses as we forgive those who trespass against us; and lead us not into temptation, but deliver us from evil. Amen.

7. Man in Paradise

God placed man in a wonderful place.
It was a pleasant place.
It was a wonderful park.
It was a beautiful garden.
It was called a paradise of pleasure.
In this paradise God placed man.
It had all kinds of trees.
They were very fair to look at.
They were beautiful.
They bore fruit.
The fruit was pleasant to eat.
In this paradise was the Tree of Life.
In this paradise was another tree.
This was the Tree of Knowledge.
The fruit of this tree gave the knowledge of good
and evil.
In this paradise was a river.
This river kept the trees and plants of paradise fresh
and beautiful.
Into this beautiful paradise God placed man.
All these wonderful and beautiful things were for him.
He was to take care of these things and keep them.
What a wonderful place!
What a beautiful place!
What love God had for Adam!

Paradise was a .... place.
Paradise was a .... park.

"Of every tree of paradise thou shalt eat: But of the tree of knowledge of good and evil, thou shalt not eat" (Gen. ii. 16–17).

Paradise was a .... garden.
Paradise had all .... of trees.
In paradise was the Tree of ....
In paradise was the Tree of ....
Tell how beautiful and wonderful paradise was.

All Things Beautiful

All things bright and beautiful
    All creatures great and small,
All things wise and wonderful —
    The Lord God made them all.

Each little flower that opens,
    Each little bird that sings —
He made their glowing colors,
    He made their tiny wings.

The purple-headed mountain,
    The river running by,
The morning and the sunset,
    That lighteth up the sky;

The tall trees in the greenwood,
    The pleasant summer sun,
The ripe fruits in the garden —
    He made them every one.

He gave us eyes to see them,
    And lips, that we might tell
How great is God Almighty,
    Who hath made all things well.
          — *John Keble*

8.   God's Command to Adam

All these wonderful and beautiful things were to be for
man for all time.

This was a great act of love.

But God forbade Adam one thing.

He told Adam: "Of every tree in paradise thou shalt
eat, but thou shalt not eat of the Tree of Knowledge."

Everything in paradise was for Adam except this Tree
of Knowledge.

God told Adam what would happen if he did eat of the
Tree of Knowledge.

But if Adam did eat of the fruit of the Tree of Knowledge, he would, as God said, "die the death."

Adam did not know what death was. He was to live
forever, if he kept God's command.

What was God's command to Adam?
What would happen to Adam if he did not keep God's
commandment?
Would you have kept God's command?

9.   God Creates Eve

God saw man alone in paradise.

He said that it was not good for man to be alone.

"Let Us," God said, "make him a helper like himself."

God made Eve.

Adam went fast asleep.

He was in a deep sleep.

God took one of his ribs.

From it God made Eve.

Adam said, "She is bone of my bone. She is flesh of my flesh."

God made man from the slime of the earth.

God made woman from man's body.

Man and wife are of one flesh.

Who said,
 "Let Us make him a helper like himself"?
 "She is bone of my bone. She is flesh of my flesh"?
To whom was it said?
How was Eve made?
Man and wife are .... flesh.

10. Adam Disobeys God

Adam had everything in paradise except the fruit of the Tree of Knowledge.

Adam and Eve ate of the other fruits.

These fruits were always ready for Adam and Eve.

They did not have to work to raise the fruits.

They were happy.

They did not know death.

But the devil disguised as a serpent said to Eve: "You shall not die the death if you eat of the Tree of Knowledge."

The serpent told her what would happen if she did eat of the Tree of Knowledge.

He promised her that her eyes would be opened.

He promised more. "You shall be as God, knowing good and knowing evil."

The devil was wrong.

Eve was weak.

She was tempted.

She looked at the Tree of Knowledge.

The tree was fair and beautiful to her eyes.

The fruit of the tree seemed good to eat.

She was tempted more.

She ate of the Tree of Knowledge.

She gave Adam the fruit to eat.

He did eat, too.

He knew evil.

He disobeyed God's command.

He sinned.

He sins who disobeys the command of God.

We sin when we disobey the commands of God.

Who said, "Of every tree in paradise thou shalt eat, but thou
  shalt not eat of the Tree of Knowledge"? (Lesson 8)

To whom was it said?

Who said, "You shall not die if you eat of the Tree of
  Knowledge"?

To whom was it said?

Who said, "You shall be as God, knowing good and knowing
  evil"?

To whom was it said?

Adam was forbidden to eat of the Tree of . . . .

Whom did the devil tempt?

What promise did he make?

Eve ate the forbidden fruit of the . . . . of . . . .

Eve gave . . . . the fruit of the tree.

Adam . . . . , too.

Did Adam sin? Why? When do we sin?

11. Adam Is Punished

Adam was afraid.

He knew evil.

He sinned.

God knew Eve tempted Adam.

God knew the serpent tempted Eve.

God said to the serpent, "Upon thy breast thou shalt go. Thou shalt eat the earth all the days of thy life."

God told Eve that her sorrows would be many, and she would suffer much.

To Adam, God said, "Thou hast listened to thy wife, and didst eat of the tree, which I commanded thee that thou shouldst not eat. Because of that, thou shalt labor and work all the days of thy life for thy food. In the sweat of thy face thou shalt eat bread till thou return to the earth from which thou wert made."

God said to Adam: "For dust thou art, and to dust thou shalt return."

Man's body made from the slime of the earth, will return to the earth, but when it goes to Heaven after death it will be made glorious.

But a great thing happened. God promised that from among the children of Eve there would be born the Savior of men, the Redeemer. This is the promise that Jesus Christ would come to save men from the results of Adam's disobedience.

Who said, "Thou shalt eat the earth all the days of thy life"? To whom was it said?

[23]

"I will put enmities between thee and the woman, and thy seed and her seed: she shall crush thy head" (Gen. iii. 15).

Who said, "In the sweat of thy face shalt thou eat bread"?
To whom was it said?
Who said, "For dust thou art, and into dust thou shalt return"?
To whom was it said?
God knew the devil tempted . . . .
God knew Eve tempted . . . .
What was the punishment of the serpent?
What was the punishment of Eve?
What was the punishment of Adam?
What promise was made by God?
Who is the Savior of men?

12. Grace, the Life of the Soul

Man has a living soul.

It was the grace of God that gave life to the soul.

This grace is called sanctifying grace, because it sanctifies the soul, or makes it holy.

The soul of Adam was beautiful in every way because it had this grace of God.

It could understand more easily than we do.

It could understand more clearly than we do.

It had a stronger will to do things than we have.

It could do things more easily than we do.

The soul of Adam because of his disobedience lost the grace of God. His body was to learn what death is.

We call this loss of grace by the soul of Adam, original sin.

When we are born our souls are without this grace of God. We are born in original sin.

Our soul is like Adam's after he disobeyed God's law.

The soul of Adam could not understand so easily as it did before.

It could not understand so clearly as it did.

Its will was not so strong to do things as it was before.

Its will did not find it so easy to do things it wished to do.

This happened to the souls of all the children of Adam.

Every child that is born is without this grace.

An easy way to give this grace to the soul of every child and every person has been opened.

It was made possible by the Redeemer Whom God had promised to Adam.

It was Adam who brought original sin to man.

It was through Christ Jesus that original sin is washed away and grace is restored to the soul.

We shall learn how.

. . . . is the life of the soul.

Name three things about the soul of Adam before his disobedience.

What happened to Adam's soul because of his disobedience?

What is true of the soul of all persons who are born?

The lack of grace in our soul at birth is called . . . . sin.

We are born with . . . . in our soul.

We are born in original . . . .

We can secure . . . . easily.

This is possible through . . . . , our Redeemer.

In this way the promise to . . . . was kept.

13.   Man, a Pilgrim on the Road to Heaven

God sent Adam out of the paradise of pleasure.

The beautiful things of paradise were his no more.

The wonderful things of paradise were his no more.

He was sent forth to work the earth.

He went forth to earn his bread in the sweat of his brow.

His soul was not so strong.

It was made stronger by his sorrow for his disobedience and by a pure love of God.

Adam was to learn what death is.

Every man and every woman has learned or will learn what it is.

Every person is in this world on the road from life to death.

Every person hopes after death to return to God.

Every person hopes to go to his home in Heaven with God.

That is the true home of the soul.

Whether man goes there will depend on what man does on the road from birth to death.

If he loves God purely, he will arrive at his place in Heaven with God.

Man is a pilgrim on the road of life. And Heaven is the real end of his journey.

What a wonderful end of a journey!

That will be like Adam's paradise of pleasure.

There will be no tears there.

There will be no sorrow there.
There will be no crying there.
There will be no mourning there.
There will be no death there.
There will be everlasting life.
And God will wipe the tears from all eyes.

What did Adam do after he left paradise?
.... is the true home of the soul.
Man is a .... on the road to Heaven.
How can he keep the road?   What will there be in Heaven?
Why is Heaven described by the things that are not there?

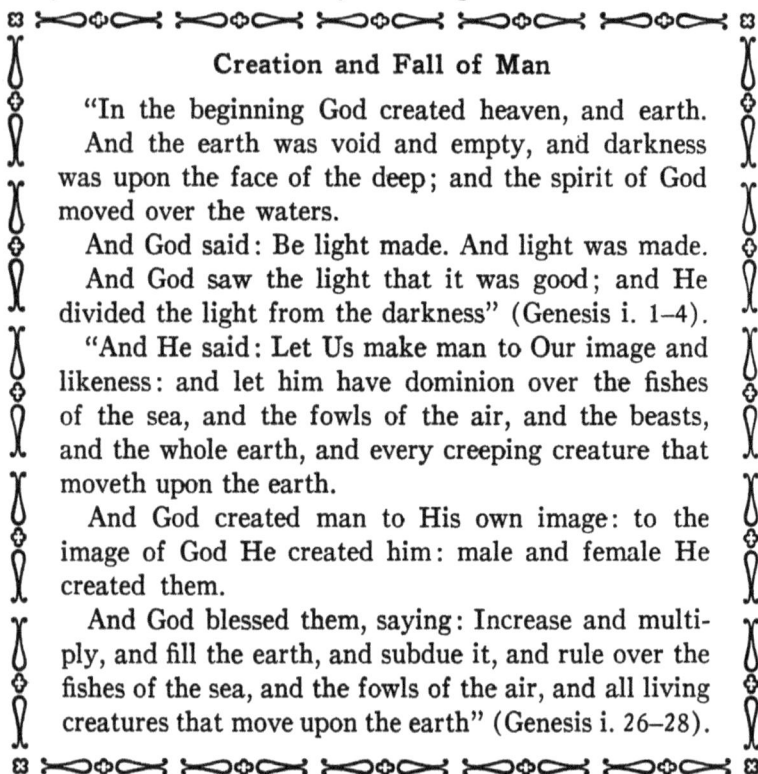

Creation and Fall of Man

"In the beginning God created heaven, and earth.

And the earth was void and empty, and darkness was upon the face of the deep; and the spirit of God moved over the waters.

And God said: Be light made. And light was made.

And God saw the light that it was good; and He divided the light from the darkness" (Genesis i. 1–4).

"And He said: Let Us make man to Our image and likeness: and let him have dominion over the fishes of the sea, and the fowls of the air, and the beasts, and the whole earth, and every creeping creature that moveth upon the earth.

And God created man to His own image: to the image of God He created him: male and female He created them.

And God blessed them, saying: Increase and multiply, and fill the earth, and subdue it, and rule over the fishes of the sea, and the fowls of the air, and all living creatures that move upon the earth" (Genesis i. 26–28).

14. Christian Doctrine Review

The Creation

1. Who created you?
   God created me.
2. Who made the world?
   God made the world.
3. Who is God?
   God is the Creator of Heaven and earth, and of all things.
4. What is man?
   Man is a creature composed of body and soul and made to the image and likeness of God.
5. Is this likeness in the body or in the soul?
   The likeness is chiefly in the soul.
6. Why did God make you?
   God made me to know Him, to love Him, and to serve Him in this world, and to be happy with Him forever in the next.
7. Of which must we take more care, our soul or our body?
   We must take more care of our soul than of our body.
8. Why must we take more care of our soul than of our body?
   We must take more care of our soul than of our body, because in losing our soul we lose God and everlasting happiness.
9. What is God?
   God is a spirit infinitely perfect.
10. Had God a beginning?
    God had no beginning; He always was and He always will be.
11. Where is God?
    God is everywhere.

12. Does God know all things?
   God knows all things, even our most secret thoughts, words, and actions.
13. Who were the first man and woman?
   The first man and woman were Adam and Eve.
14. Were Adam and Eve innocent and holy when they came from the hand of God?
   Adam and Eve were innocent and holy when they came from the hand of God.
15. Did God give any command to Adam and Eve?
   To try their obedience God commanded Adam and Eve not to eat of a certain fruit which grew in the garden of paradise.
16. Did Adam and Eve remain faithful to God?
   Adam and Eve did not remain faithful to God, but broke His command by eating the forbidden fruit.
17. What befell Adam and Eve on account of their sin?
   Adam and Eve on account of their sin lost innocence and holiness, and were doomed to sickness and death.
18. What is the sin called which we inherit from our first parents?
   The sin which we inherit from our first parents is called original sin.
19. Why is this sin called original?
   This sin is called original because it comes down to us from our first parents, and we are brought into the world with its guilt on our soul.
20. Did God abandon man after he fell into sin?
   God did not abandon man after he fell into sin, but promised him a Redeemer, Who was to satisfy for man's sin and reopen to him the gates of heaven.

The Ten Commandments

1. I am the Lord thy God, Thou shalt not have strange gods before Me.

2. Thou shalt not take the name of the Lord thy God in vain.

3. Remember that thou keep holy the Sabbath day.

4. Honor thy father and thy mother, that it may be well with thee, and thou mayest live long on earth.

5. Thou shalt not kill.

6. Thou shalt not commit adultery.

7. Thou shalt not steal.

8. Thou shalt not bear false witness against thy neighbor.

9. Thou shalt not covet thy neighbor's wife.

10. Thou shalt not covet thy neighbor's goods.

II. The Commandments of God

15. Obey the Commandments

God wanted to help man.

God did not abandon man after Adam's sin.

He wanted man to stay on the road which leads to Heaven.

God gave him some guideposts.

These are His Commandments.

We must obey them.

The soul knows that.

If we do not obey them, what happened to Adam will happen to us.

Adam's soul lost the grace of God.

It lost its supernatural life.

So if we disobey as Adam did, we shall lose God's grace.

If we are truly sorry for disobeying God's Commandment, we can regain God's grace, and life will be restored to the soul.

God punishes in Hell those who do not keep His Commandments in important matters.

God rewards those in Paradise who keep His Commandments. He fills our soul with grace here. We live with Him forever in Paradise. So great is the reward of keeping His Commandments.

If we keep God's Commandments our souls will have God's grace. The Commandments of God are a great help to us on the road to our home with God.

"He wrote them in two tables of stone, which He delivered unto me" (Deut. v. 22).

Man is a pilgrim on the road.

Are there any guideposts on the road?

What are they?

Will they help us keep the road?

If we do not keep the Commandments, God punishes us in . . . .

If we do keep the Commandments, we will live with God forever in . . . .

If we are truly sorry for our disobedience to God's Commandments, what will happen?

16.   The Ten Commandments of God

Adam sinned when he disobeyed God's Commandments.

I sin if I disobey God's law or His Commandments.

You sin if you disobey God's law or Commandments.

We all sin if we disobey God's law or Commandments.

Has God given Commandments for me to obey the way He did for Adam?

Yes, God has given Commandments for me to obey just as He did for Adam.

What are these Commandments?

They are the Commandments given to Moses on Mount Sinai.

They were binding on the Jews.

They are binding on all men and women.

They are binding on you and on me.

They are binding on all boys and all girls, on all men and all women.

They are binding on every person, big or small, young or old, who knows what they are about.

[34]

This means on all persons who are about seven years or older.

Christ said that if you would have life or grace in your soul, you must keep the Commandments.

It is our *duty* to learn what these Commandments are, and what they mean.

The Ten Commandments of God given to Moses on Mount Sinai, and binding on every person are:

1. *I am the Lord thy God. Thou shalt not have strange gods before Me.*
2. *Thou shalt not take the name of the Lord thy God in vain.*
3. *Remember thou keep holy the Sabbath Day.*
4. *Honor thy father and thy mother.*
5. *Thou shalt not kill.*
6. *Thou shalt not commit adultery.*
7. *Thou shalt not steal.*
8. *Thou shalt not bear false witness against thy neighbor.*
9. *Thou shalt not covet thy neighbor's wife.*
10. *Thou shalt not covet thy neighbor's goods.*

Do you know these Commandments of God?

The first three Commandments govern our love of God.

The other seven Commandments govern our love of our neighbor.

God told the Jews and through them, all men, to keep these words in their hearts.

They should tell them to their children.

They should think about the words of God at all times — in the day, at night, at home, or on a journey.

They should be kept before the eyes.

This we should do, too, whether we are young or old. We can do this best by loving God.

"Thou shalt," says Christ, "love the Lord thy God with thy whole heart, and with thy whole soul, and with thy whole strength, and with all thy mind."

Adam sinned when he .... God's Commandment.

I .... when I disobey God's Commandment.

God's Commandments are binding on all ....

God's Commandments are binding on you and on ....

God's Commandments are .... in number.

What is the First Commandment of God?

What is the Second Commandment of God?

What is the Third Commandment of God?

What is the Fourth Commandment of God?

What is the Fifth Commandment of God?

What is the Sixth Commandment of God?

What is the Seventh Commandment of God?

What is the Eighth Commandment of God?

What is the Ninth Commandment of God?

What is the Tenth Commandment of God?

The first three Commandments relate to the love of ....

The other seven Commandments relate to the love of ....

17. How to Keep the Commandments

"If you would have life or grace," Christ said, "keep the Commandments."

How can I keep the Commandments is a question my soul always asks.

I want to keep the Commandments.

I want to gain eternal life.

I want, at the end of the road, to find my home with God.

How can I do it?

"Keep the Commandments," is the simple answer.

How can I keep before my soul these Commandments every day and every time I am tempted?

Let us see what questions we can keep before our souls to keep us from being tempted, or in time of temptation to keep God's Commandments before us.

The pure love of God will always save us.

Who said, "If you would have life keep the Commandments"?

Keep the Commandments and you will gain . . . . life.

Keep the Commandments and you will reach your last home with . . . .

Keep the . . . . and you will have . . . . in your soul.

The pure love of God will help you keep the . . . . of God.

"Good Master, what good shall I do that I may have life
everlasting?" (Matt. xix. 16; Luke xviii. 18.)

18. The Pure Love of God

Love of God is the greatest thing in religion.

The soul wishes to be united to God in love.

The soul wishes to keep away from those persons or places or things which take the soul away from God.

These are some of the questions which the soul wishing to stay close to God keeps before it. This keeps the soul on God's highway.

The First Commandment is: *I am the Lord thy God. Thou shalt not have strange gods before Me.*

Do I often show my faith in God?

Do I often show my love of God?

Do I often show my trust in God?

Do I say little prayers to God in the morning?

Do I say little prayers to God at night?

Do I say little prayers to God whenever I have a bad thought or want to do something that is not just right?

I love God. I trust God. I hope in God.

Dreams cannot tell us what is going to happen.

Only God knows that. He knows all things.

The Second Commandment also relates to the love of God: It is: *Thou shalt not take the name of the Lord thy God in vain.*

We can keep the Second Commandment if we will keep in mind the following questions:

Do I use the name of God reverently only?

Do I use the name of God when I am angry, or as the other boys and girls say, "When I am mad"?

Do I use the name of God when I do not need to about little things?

The Third Commandment points out a way we may pay our respect to God and show our love for Him. This Commandment is: *Remember thou keep holy the Sabbath day.*

Do I go to Mass every Sunday?

Do I go to Mass every holyday of obligation?

Do I try to make Sunday holy and happy?

Do I do any work that is not necessary on Sundays or holydays?

Do I think of God on Sundays?

Do I think of God every day?

These three Commandments teach us to love God.

If I am loyal to God . . . .
1. I shall show my . . . . in God.
2. I shall show my . . . . of God.
3. I shall say little . . . . to God, in the morning and at night.
4. I shall say little . . . . to God whenever I have a bad thought or want to do something that is not right.

What questions can I ask myself to help me keep the First Commandment of God?

What questions can I ask myself to help me keep the Second Commandment of God?

What questions can I ask myself to help me keep the Third Commandment of God?

What three Commandments teach us to love God?

What is the First Commandment of God?

What is the Second Commandment of God?

What is the Third Commandment of God?

Different Ways

Dear God, I try to tell You
Through all the livelong day
"I love You!" And to say it
In every sort of way.
I say it in the morning
By jumping out of bed
Just when I ought to do it
You know, dear God, instead
Of lying there and thinking
How comfy beds can be —
For that would not be loving
You, God — but loving me!
And then I say "I love You!"
By washing as I should,
And all day long I say it
By trying to be good.
"I love You, God! I love You!"
There are as many ways
Of saying that I love You
As there are nights and days!
— *Mary Dixon Thayer*

He Prayeth Best

"He prayeth well, who loveth well
Both man and bird and beast.

He prayeth best, who loveth best
All things both great and small;
For the dear God who loveth us,
He made and loveth all."
— *Samuel Taylor Coleridge*

[41]

19. Love of Neighbor

We must love our neighbor.

We must love our neighbor for the love of God.

We are all His creatures.

He is our Father.

We are all children of God.

How can we be sure we love our neighbor?

How can we be sure we serve our neighbor?

Let the soul keep questions before it to keep alive the love of neighbor and the love of God.

The Fourth Commandment is: *Honor thy father and thy mother*. Let us begin with those creatures of God who are closest to us: our mother and father.

Do I love them?

Do I obey them promptly?

Do I help mother?

Do I try to find things to do for mother and for father?

Do I obey the law?

Do I obey my teachers?

The Fifth Commandment forbids us to injure our neighbor.

It also requires us to love our neighbor.

It says only *Thou shalt not kill*.

Have I injured mother or father?

Have I injured brother and sister?

Have I injured other children?

Have I injured or hurt other people?

Do I pick quarrels with anyone?

Have I a temper? Do I control it?

The Sixth Commandment is: *Thou shalt not commit adultery.*

The Ninth Commandment is: *Thou shalt not covet thy neighbor's wife.*

The Sixth and Ninth Commandments forbid us to do, say, read, or think about anything that is immodest.

These two Commandments require us also to love our neighbor.

Do I think about beautiful things?

Do I let evil thoughts stay in my mind?

The Seventh Commandment forbids us to take or to want unjustly anything that belongs to our neighbor.

The Seventh Commandment says only — *Thou shalt not steal.*

The Tenth Commandment forbids the same things. It forbids our desiring to possess unjustly such things as belong to our neighbor.

The Tenth Commandment is: *Thou shalt not covet thy neighbor's goods.*

The Seventh and Tenth Commandments require us to love our neighbor and respect his property.

Do I take things that do not belong to me?

Do I keep things that I borrow a long time?

Do I mark up school books?

Do I mark up books I borrow?

Do I injure school property?

Do I injure my neighbor's property?

The Eighth Commandment forbids us to lie or tell a falsehood about our neighbor.

The Eighth Commandment requires us to love our neighbor.

This Commandment is: *Thou shalt not bear false witness against thy neighbor.*

Do I ever tell lies about my friends?

Do I ever tell lies about anyone?

Do I tell truths about other children that should not be repeated?

Do I fail to say good things about other children whenever I can?

Do I keep silent when a good word would help another child?

These seven Commandments will help us love our neighbor. If we keep these Commandments, it will show we love God, too.

The world would be much happier if all people would try to keep the Ten Commandments.

What Commandments teach us the love of neighbor?

Name three good reasons why we should love our neighbor.

What is the Fourth Commandment of God?

What is the Fifth Commandment of God?

What is the Sixth Commandment of God?

What is the Seventh Commandment of God?

What is the Eighth Commandment of God?

What is the Ninth Commandment of God?

What is the Tenth Commandment of God?

What questions kept in mind will help the soul honor father and mother?

What questions kept in mind will help the soul to respect the life of our neighbor?

What questions kept in mind will help the soul act modestly toward our neighbor?

What questions kept in mind will help the soul act rightly toward the property of our neighbor?

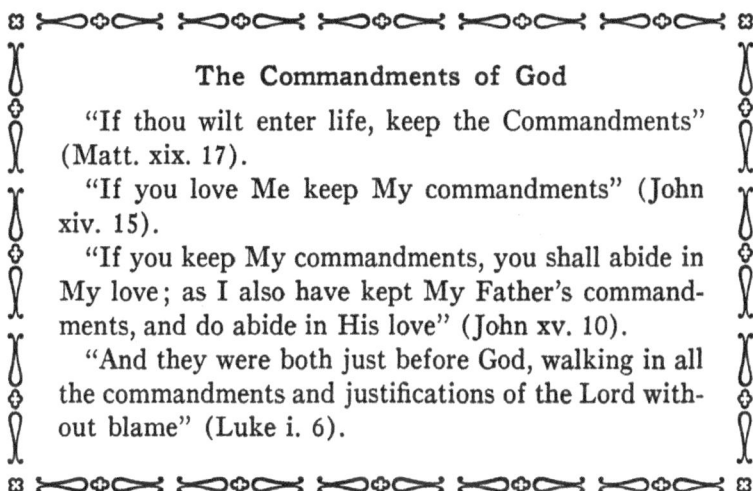

The Commandments of God

"If thou wilt enter life, keep the Commandments" (Matt. xix. 17).

"If you love Me keep My commandments" (John xiv. 15).

"If you keep My commandments, you shall abide in My love; as I also have kept My Father's commandments, and do abide in His love" (John xv. 10).

"And they were both just before God, walking in all the commandments and justifications of the Lord without blame" (Luke i. 6).

Christian Doctrine Review

The Commandments

21. Which are the Commandments that contain the whole law of God?

The Commandments which contain the whole law of God are these two: First, thou shalt love the Lord thy God with thy whole heart, with thy whole soul, with thy whole strength, and with thy whole mind; Second, thou shalt love thy neighbor as thyself.

22. Why do these two Commandments of the love of God and of our neighbor contain the whole law of God?

These two Commandments of the love of God and of our neighbor contain the whole law of God because all the other Commandments are given either to help us to keep these two, or to direct us how to shun what is opposed to them.

23. Which are the Commandments of God?

The Commandments of God are these ten:

1. I am the Lord thy God, Who brought thee out of the land of Egypt, out of the house of bondage. Thou shalt not have strange gods before Me. Thou shalt not make to thyself a graven thing, nor the likeness of any thing that is in heaven above, or in the earth beneath, nor of those things that are in the waters under the earth. Thou shalt not adore them, nor serve them.

2. Thou shalt not take the name of the Lord thy God in vain.

3. Remember thou keep holy the Sabbath Day.

4. Honor thy father and thy mother.

5. Thou shalt not kill.

6. Thou shalt not commit adultery.

7. Thou shalt not steal.

8. Thou shalt not bear false witness against thy neighbor.

9. Thou shalt not covet thy neighbor's wife.

10. Thou shalt not covet thy neighbor's goods.

24. Who gave the Ten Commandments?

God Himself gave the Ten Commandments to Moses on Mount Sinai, and Christ our Lord confirmed them.

III. Christ the Redeemer

21. The Promise of God Fulfilled

God gave man the Commandments to help man on the road to Heaven.

But God did more for us.

He promised to Adam a Savior, or Redeemer, Who would save all men.

A long time after this the Savior came.

He was the Son of God.

The Son of God became man. His name was Jesus.

He came to save us from the effects of Adam's sin.

He came to save us from original sin.

An Angel announced to Mary that she was to be the Mother of God. She was to be the Mother of Jesus.

Jesus was born in a stable in Bethlehem of Mary, the Virgin.

He was conceived of the Holy Ghost.

His foster father was Joseph, the carpenter.

Angels announced to the shepherds the birth of their Savior, Jesus Christ.

The child was born as the angels announced.

After eight days He was given the name of Jesus. He was later brought to the temple or church as the laws of the Jews required.

Wise men in the East saw His star and came to worship Him, and they brought Him wonderful gifts.

"And thou Bethlehem, out of thee shall come forth the
captain that shall rule My people Israel" (Matt. ii. 6).

Herod, the king, wished to kill Him, but an angel warned Joseph to take the Mother and the Child to Egypt. Joseph did.

An angel told Joseph of Herod's death so that Joseph, the Mother, and the Child could return.

The Child Jesus was brought regularly to Jerusalem.

When Jesus was twelve years old a strange thing happened. Joseph, Mary, and Jesus went to Jerusalem. They went to the temple to pray. They were ready to return home. Joseph and Mary began their return journey to Nazareth. They thought that Jesus was with relatives. They found out He was not. They returned to Jerusalem.

Mary found Jesus with the learned men. They were called doctors — doctors of the law. They knew the laws of religion very well indeed. These men were greatly surprised at the learning and wisdom of the Child Jesus.

The Bible says, "They were astonished at His wisdom and His answers."

Mary and Joseph returned home happy with the Child Jesus.

And Jesus grew in wisdom and age and grace with God and man.

God promised for man a . . . . or . . . .

The Son of God is the . . . . or . . . .

. . . . is His name.

He was born of the Virgin . . . .

He was conceived of the . . . .

"Hail, full of grace, the Lord is with thee: blessed art thou among women" (Luke i. 28).

His foster father was . . . .
Herod wanted to kill . . . .
Joseph took Mary and . . . . to Egypt.
After Herod died, Joseph brought Mary and . . . .
  from . . . .
Jesus was born in . . . .
Jesus lived in . . . .
Tell about the Wise Men of the East.
Tell what the Angels did in this story.
Tell what Jesus did in the temple.

The Lamb

Little lamb, who made thee?
Dost thou know who made thee,
Gave thee life and bade thee feed
By the stream and o'er the mead;
Gave thee clothing of delight,
Softest clothing, woolly, bright;
Gave thee such a tender voice,
Making all the vales rejoice?
Little lamb, who made thee?
Dost thou know who made thee?

Little lamb, I'll tell thee;
Little lamb, I'll tell thee;
He is called by thy name,
For He calls Himself a lamb.
He is meek and He is mild,
He became a little Child.
I a child, and thou a lamb,
We are called by His name,
Little lamb, God bless thee!
Little lamb, God bless thee!

—William Blake

"And the Child grew, and waxed strong, full of wisdom,
and the grace of God was in Him" (Luke ii. 40).

22. Mary, Mother of God

Mary was the Mother of Jesus.

The angel of God told Mary this would happen before it did happen.

She was happy.

She was happy to be the Mother of Jesus Who was God come down from Heaven. He became Man to save us.

Mary is the Mother of God.

She was the only human creature born without original sin. This is called the Immaculate Conception.

She did not sin in her life. Her soul was most pure.

She is Mary, most holy.

She is, too, Queen of Heaven.

She is near God, the Father, in Heaven.

She is near her Blessed Son, too.

She is near to God, the Holy Ghost.

She helps us with God.

She presents our prayers.

Pray to her for her help.

Mary, Mother of God, pray for us.

Mary, most holy, pray for us.

Mary, Queen of Heaven, pray for us.

Mary, full of grace, pray for us.

Mary, Mother of all Christians, pray for us.

Mary is the .... of ....
Jesus is the Son of ....
.... is the Mother of God.

[53]

Mary was born without . . . . sin.
Mary did not . . . . during her life.
Mary is . . . . of Heaven.
Mary can help us with God.
Say five little prayers to Mary.
Make one prayer of your own.

A Prayer to Mary

Dear Mother, pray for me,
    That God's grace in me dwell;
Of Jesus ask this boon:
    That I may love Him well.

God's Mother, pray for me,
    This year and all my days;
So I may come to Heaven,
    And thee and Jesus praise.
                    — *Father H. G. Hughes*

The Divine Praises

Blessed be God.
Blessed be His holy name.
Blessed be Jesus Christ, true God and true Man.
Blessed be the name of Jesus.
Blessed be His most Sacred Heart.
Blessed be Jesus in the most Holy Sacrament of the altar.
Blessed be the great Mother of God, Mary most holy.
Blessed be her holy and immaculate conception.
Blessed be the name of Mary, Virgin and Mother.
Blessed be St. Joseph, her most chaste spouse.
Blessed be God in His angels and in His saints.

[54]

HAIL Mary, full of grace! The Lord is with thee: blessed art thou among women, and blessed is the fruit of thy womb, JESUS

HOLY Mary, Mother of GOD, pray for us sinners, now and at the hour of our death. Amen.

"And behold a voice from heaven, saying: This is My beloved Son, in whom I am well pleased" (Matt. iii. 17).

24. The Blessed Trinity

Jesus grew to be a man.

He was thirty years old when John baptized Him in the water of the River Jordan. This John is called John the Baptist.

The Holy Ghost appeared in the form of a dove.

The voice of God, the Father, was heard from a cloud, saying: "This is My beloved Son in Whom I am well pleased."

There were present at the Baptism of Jesus, the three Persons of the Blessed Trinity:

> God the Father,
> God the Son,
> God the Holy Ghost.

There is one God in three Divine Persons.

They have one nature. They are one.

We call this fact to mind every time we bless ourselves, when we say "In the name of the Father, and of the Son, and of the Holy Ghost."

God the Father is the First Person of the Blessed Trinity.

God the Son is the Second Person of the Blessed Trinity.

God the Holy Ghost is the Third Person of the Blessed Trinity.

There is only one God, but there are three Persons in God.

This is hard to understand, but it is true.

Christ has told us.

Jesus was .... years old when he was baptized.

John baptized ....

At the baptism of Christ the .... appeared as a dove.

At the baptism of Christ the .... of .... was heard from a cloud.

The Blessed Trinity is one ....

The Blessed Trinity is one God in .... Divine Persons.

The three Divine Persons are:

        God the ....

        God the ....

        God the ....

God the Father is the .... Person of the Blessed Trinity.

God the Son is the .... Person of the Blessed Trinity.

God the Holy Ghost is the .... Person of the Blessed Trinity.

How are we reminded of the Blessed Trinity when we bless ourselves?

The Blessed Trinity

O blessed Trinity!
Thy children dare
To lift their hearts to Thee,
And bless Thy triple Majesty!
Holy Trinity!
Blessed Equal Three,
One God, we praise Thee.
—*Father Faber*

25. The Miracles of Christ

Christ lived for three years after His baptism by John.

He did many wonderful things.

He had the power of God, because He was God.

He performed miracles.

He walked on the waters.

Even the winds obeyed Him.

He stilled a storm.

He healed the sick by His word only.

He made the blind see.

He made the lame walk.

He cured lepers.

He raised men from the dead.

He turned bread and wine into His body and blood by His word only.

He, Himself, rose from the dead.

He appeared for forty days afterwards to His disciples.

He ascended into Heaven.

He sits at the right hand of God.

He is indeed the Son of God.

Christ, by the power of God, performed . . . .

He walked the . . . .

He . . . . the sick by His word only.

He made the blind . . . .

He made the lame . . . .

He cured . . . .

He raised men from the . . . .

He, Himself, rose from the . . . .

Christ is the . . . . of God.

Christ sits at the right . . . . of God in Heaven.

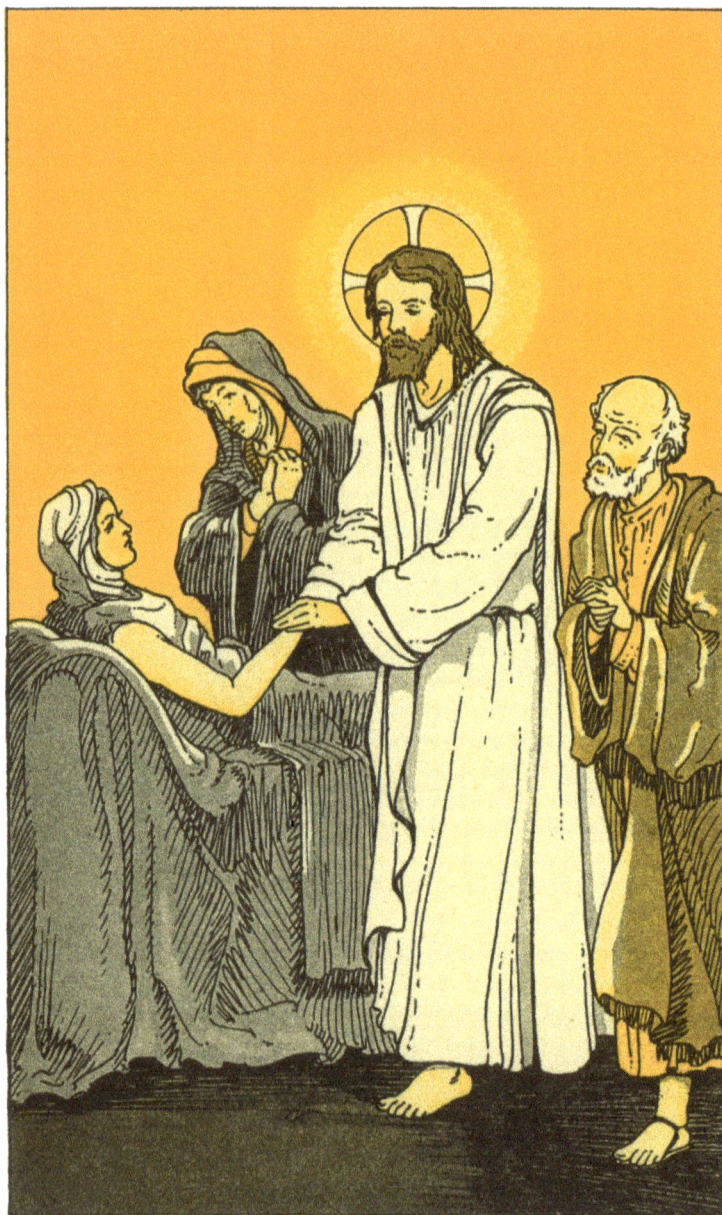

"The damsel is not dead, but sleepeth. . . . Damsel
(I say to thee), arise" (Mark v. 39, 41).

26. Christ Loved Men

Christ went about doing good works.

He went about teaching wonderful things about the Kingdom of Heaven.

He went about teaching men how to live good lives.

He loved men and women.

He loved boys and girls.

He wished to serve them.

He wished to help them to know God better.

He wished men and women to keep the Commandments of God.

He wished boys and girls to keep the Commandments of God.

He loved boys and girls.

He loved children.

There is a story in the Bible that shows Christ's love of children.

The leaders among Christ's disciples we call the Apostles.

There were twelve of them. Peter was the leader of them.

Children were pressing to get near to Christ: The Apostles thought Christ was tired. They tried to keep the children away. But Christ would not have it so.

Christ said to His Apostles: "Suffer little children to come unto Me, and forbid them not, for of such is the Kingdom of Heaven."

"Suffer children to come to Me, and forbid them not:
for of such is the kingdom of God" (Luke xviii. 16).

What are some of the things Christ did on earth?

He loved all of .... creatures.

He loved .... and women.

He loved boys and ....

He wanted us to .... God better.

He wanted us to keep the .... of God.

Tell one story of Christ's love of children from the Bible.

27. The Holy Eucharist

The Jews celebrated a great feast every year.

They offered up a lamb to God. They were commanded
to do this. It reminded them, too, of God's love for
them and of all that He did for them when they were
in Egypt. He brought them into the Promised Land.

This feast is called the feast of the Pasch or the
Passover.

Christ wished to keep this feast.

He told the Apostles that He was to die shortly.

He told them that He would rise again from the dead.

The Jewish priests were plotting against Him.

Judas was to betray Him.

These things He knew.

He knows all things.

That first Holy Thursday night He was to keep the
old Jewish feast.

He would then and there establish a new feast for
the New Law.

The Apostles were gathered together to keep the feast.

At that time He established the Holy Eucharist.

"This is My Body. This is My Blood."

He took bread in His holy hands. He blessed it and broke it and gave it to His followers or disciples.

He said to them: "Take ye and eat. This is My Body."

The disciples ate. They received not bread but the Body of Christ.

Christ Who did so many wonderful things could do this. This is perhaps His greatest miracle. But Christ is God, and for Him nothing is impossible.

Christ then took the cup or chalice in His holy hands. He gave thanks to His Father.

He gave the chalice to the disciples, saying: "Drink ye all of this, for this is My Blood."

The disciples drank, and they drank the Blood of our Lord.

They received the Body and Blood of Christ.

This was the first Mass with Christ Himself as Priest.

He told the Apostles, "Do this in commemoration of Me."

Ever since, the Apostles and their successors have said the Holy Mass as Christ told them.

Christ offered His Body and Blood under the appearance of bread and wine in this first Mass on this first Holy Thursday night. This was an unbloody sacrifice.

On the next day, Good Friday, Christ was to offer His life on the cross. He died on the cross. This was the bloody sacrifice which Christ offered.

This was the same sacrifice as on Holy Thursday night.

This is the same sacrifice as is offered every day in Holy Mass.

Christ, the Son of God, gave His priests power to change in the Mass, the bread and wine into His Body and Blood.

This happens at every Mass, by the power of Christ, acting through the priest.

In Holy Communion we receive not bread but the Body and Blood of Christ.

This is a mystery. We do not understand this, but we know it is true because Christ told us so.

This is a great source of grace which is the life of the soul. It comes from the source of all grace, God Himself.

Though the host or bread in Holy Communion may *seem* like bread, it is not. It is the Body and Blood of Christ.

It appears to be bread, but it is not. It is the Body and Blood of Christ.

This Body and Blood of Christ is the food of the soul. It is spiritual food, not like ordinary bread, or ordinary food.

From this spiritual food comes grace which is the life of the soul.

O Jesus, come into my heart and make a good child of me.

Christ wished to keep the Jewish .... of the ....
Christ established a new .... on this very night.
Christ established the ....

Who was present?

What is the day called?

What did Christ do with the bread?

What did He say?

What happened?

What did Christ do with the wine?

What did He say?

What happened?

Christ gave power to priests to change in the . . . . the bread and wine into His Body and Blood.

When does this happen?

The Holy Communion we receive is not bread but the . . . . and . . . . of Jesus Christ.

Holy Communion is a source of . . . .

Grace comes from . . . .

Christ instituted the . . . .

We receive the Body and Blood of Christ in the Sacrament of . . . .

The Body and Blood of Christ is the . . . . of the soul.

Make a brief prayer such as is given in the last sentence of this story.

"And bearing His own cross, He went forth to that place
which is called Calvary, but in Hebrew Golgotha"
(John xix. 17).

28. Christ Suffers for the Sins of Man

The Holy Eucharist is established on Holy Thursday.
That night Christ is betrayed by Judas.
Christ suffers a bloody sweat.
He is brought before the Jewish priests.
He is brought before the Roman governor, Pontius Pilate.
Pontius Pilate wants to free Jesus.
Pilate says, "I find nothing to punish Him for."
But the Jews wanted Him punished.
Then Pilate orders Jesus to be scourged.
But the Jews want Jesus crucified.
They call out, "Crucify Him, Crucify Him."
They call louder, "Crucify Him, Crucify Him."
Pilate would like to free Jesus. It is a custom to free a prisoner at this great feast.
But the Jews do not want Jesus set free.
They ask to have a thief set free.
Pilate washes his hands of the blood of the innocent man.
Christ is condemned to die.
After He is scourged, He is crowned with thorns.
He is made to carry the cross on which He is to die.
He falls a first time.
He is given some help.
He falls a second time.
He falls a third time.
His clothes are taken from Him.

"And Jesus said: Father, forgive them, for they know
not what they do. But they, dividing His garments,
cast lots" (Luke xxiii. 34).

He is nailed to the cross.

His cross is set up between two crosses each bearing a thief.

He suffers greatly.

He thirsts, and they give Him vinegar to drink.

With all His suffering, He prays for these people.

"Father," He says, "forgive them for they know not what they do."

He dies on the cross. This is Good Friday.

This happened on Mount Calvary.

He is taken down and buried in a sepulcher.

He is in the sepulcher for three days.

He rises from the dead. This is on Easter Sunday.

He appears many times after the resurrection.

He ascends into Heaven.

Christ died on the cross for our sins.

Christ died on the cross for my sins.

Christ died on the cross for my sins because He loved me.

He will save us if we love Him.

He now sits in Heaven at the right hand of the Father.

He shall judge the living and the dead.

What happened on Holy Thursday?
What happened on Good Friday?
What happened on Easter Sunday?
What happened after Easter Sunday?
Who said, "I find nothing to punish. Him for"?
To whom was it said?
Of Whom was it said?

"The Son of man shall be betrayed into the hands of men: and they shall kill Him, and the third day He shall rise again" (Matt. xvii. 21–22).

Who said, "Crucify Him, crucify Him"?
To whom was it said?
Of Whom was it said?
Who said, "Father forgive them for they know not what
  they do"?
To whom was it said?
Of whom was it said?
Christ died for our . . . .
Christ died for . . . . sins.
Look in the prayer book for the Stations of the Cross, and
  see how many of these events are pictured there.

O Sacred Cross!

O Sacred Cross! O Holy Tree!
  On which my Blessed Savior died,
Teach my poor heart the mystery
  Of my Redeemer crucified.
Cross of my Savior! Sacred Sign;
  Lead me from sin to grace divine.
          — William Cardinal O'Connell

The Way of the Cross

Along the dark aisles
  Of a chapel dim,
The little lame girl
  Drags her withered limb.

And all alone she searches
  The shadows on the walls
To find the three pictures
  Where Jesus falls.
          — Leonard Feeney, S.J.

[73]

"When He had said these things, while they looked on,
He was raised up: and a cloud received Him out of
their sight" (Acts i. 9).

29. I Believe in Jesus Christ

I believe in Jesus Christ.

His (God's) only Son, our Lord.

Who was conceived by the Holy Ghost.

Born of the Virgin Mary.

Suffered under Pontius Pilate.

Was crucified,

Died,

And was buried.

He descended into Hell.

The third day He arose again from the dead.

He ascended into Heaven,

Sitteth at the right hand of God, the Father Almighty,

From thence He shall come to judge the living and the dead.

I believe in ....

I believe He is the ...... of God.

I believe He was conceived by the ....

I believe He was born of the Virgin ....

I believe He arose from the ....

I believe He sits at the .... hand of God.

I believe He will come to .... the living and the dead.

Christ the Redeemer

"Then were little children presented to Him, that He should impose hands upon them and pray. And the disciples rebuked them.

"But Jesus said to them: Suffer the little children, and forbid them not to come to Me: for the kingdom of heaven is for such" (Matt. xix. 13, 14).

"And he that shall receive one such little child in My name, receiveth Me" (Matt. xviii. 5).

"My little children, let us not love in word, nor in tongue, but in deed, and in truth" (I John iii. 18).

"As the Father hath loved Me, I also have loved you. Abide in My love" (John xv. 9).

"Jesus answered, and said to him: If any one love Me, he will keep My word, and My Father will love him, and We will come to him, and will make Our abode with him" (John xiv. 23).

"This day is born to you a Savior Who is Christ the Lord" (Luke ii. 11).

"I am the Door. By Me if any man enter in, he shall be saved: and he shall go in and out, and shall find pastures. — I am the Good Shepherd. The Good Shepherd giveth His life for His sheep. — I am the Good Shepherd; and I know Mine, and Mine know Me" (John x. 9, 11, 14).

"I am the Way, and the Truth, and the Life. No man cometh to the Father but by Me" (John xiv. 6).

"As He was yet speaking, behold, a bright cloud overshaded them. And lo, a voice out of the cloud, saying: This is My beloved Son, in Whom I am well pleased: hear ye Him" (Matt. xvii. 5).

30. Christian Doctrine Review

Christ the Redeemer

25. Is there but one God?
    Yes; there is but one God.
26. How many persons are there in God?
    In God there are three Divine Persons, really distinct, and equal in all things — the Father, the Son, and the Holy Ghost.
27. Is the Father God?
    The Father is God and the First Person of the Blessed Trinity.
28. Is the Son God?
    The Son is God and the Second Person of the Blessed Trinity.
29. Is the Holy Ghost God?
    The Holy Ghost is God and the Third Person of the Blessed Trinity.
30. What do you mean by the Blessed Trinity?
    By the Blessed Trinity I mean one God in three Divine Persons.
31. Are the three Divine Persons equal in all things?
    The three Divine Persons are equal in all things.
32. Can we fully understand how the three Divine Persons are one and the same God?
    We cannot fully understand how the three Divine Persons are one and the same God, because this is a mystery.
33. Did God abandon man after he fell into sin?
    God did not abandon man after he fell into sin, but promised him a Redeemer, Who was to satisfy for man's sin and reopen to him the gates of Heaven.

34. Who is the Redeemer?
Our Blessed Lord and Savior, Jesus Christ, is the Redeemer of mankind.

35. What do you believe of Jesus Christ?
I believe that Jesus Christ is the Son of God, the Second Person of the Blessed Trinity, true God and true man.

36. How was the Son of God made man?
The Son of God was conceived and made man by the power of the Holy Ghost, in the womb of the Blessed Virgin Mary.

37. Was anyone ever preserved from original sin?
The Blessed Virgin Mary, through the merits of her Divine Son, was preserved free from the guilt of original sin, and this privilege is called her Immaculate Conception.

38. On what day was Christ born?
Christ was born on Christmas day in a stable at Bethlehem, over nineteen hundred years ago.

39. How long did Christ live on earth?
Christ lived on earth about thirty-three years, and led a most holy life in poverty and suffering.

40. Why did Christ live so long on earth?
Christ lived so long on earth to show us the way to Heaven by His teachings and example.

41. What did Jesus Christ suffer?
Jesus Christ suffered a bloody sweat, a cruel scourging, was crowned with thorns, and was crucified.

42. On what day did Christ die?
Christ died on Good Friday.

43. Why do you call that day "good" on which Christ died so sorrowful a death?
We call the day good on which Christ died because

by His death He showed His great love for man, and purchased for him every blessing.

44. Where did Christ die?
Christ died on Mount Calvary.

45. How did Christ die?
Christ was nailed to the cross and died on it between two thieves.

46. Why did Christ suffer and die?
Christ suffered and died for our sins.

"And suddenly there came a sound from heaven, as of a mighty wind coming. . . . And there appeared to them parted tongues as it were of fire, and it sat upon every one of them" (Acts ii. 2–3).

PART TWO

IV. The Church of Christ

31. The Roman Catholic Church

Christ, the Son of God, became man and died on the cross to save all men.

He came to save or redeem men in all ages.

He came to save Jews and Gentiles, rich and poor, men and women, boys and girls. He came to save everyone. He came to save you and me.

He became a man, and His death as a man was part of His plan to save all men. He died for us.

He had a plan to continue His work after His ascension to Heaven.

He would establish His Church to continue His work on earth. He did establish it. It is the Roman Catholic Church. The Apostles were its first bishops and priests. Peter was the first Pope.

Christ promised His Church would last forever. He would send to it the Holy Ghost, the third Person of the Blessed Trinity. The Holy Ghost would remain with it forever. He would teach it truth. It could not be led into error. The Church would teach men in all ages, and the Holy Ghost would save it from error.

The Holy Ghost came upon the Apostles on that first Pentecost day, fifty days after the Resurrection.

The Pope is Bishop of Rome, the Vicar of Christ,
the successor of Peter, the visible head of the
Roman Catholic Church.

"And there appeared to them parted tongues of fire and It sat on every one of them."

The Roman Catholic Church was established by Christ on that first Pentecost day. We call Pentecost its birthday.

It has had about nineteen hundred birthdays since then. It will last until the end of time as Christ promised. It lives today. It is our Church. It is the only Christian Church which goes back to Christ as its founder.

In it we live the life of Christ. We receive through it the seven sacraments Christ Himself established.

We call the Church our Holy Mother Church. To it we should go as a child goes to its mother for help, for consolation, in prayer. To it we go, too, for those sacraments which are the life of the soul.

Christ Himself made a great promise to the Church. These are His words:

"Whosoever heareth you heareth Me, and he that despiseth you despiseth Me."

Why did Christ become man?
Christ died to save .... men.
How did Christ plan to continue His work of saving men?
.... establish the Roman Catholic Church.
.... is the birthday of the Church.
On Pentecost the Holy Ghost appeared to the .... as parted tongues of ...., and sat upon every one of them.
Who were its first bishops and priests?
Who was the first Pope?
Who is Pope today?
Who is your bishop or archbishop?

[83]

Who is your pastor?
The Roman Catholic Church will last . . . .
The Holy Ghost will remain with the Roman Catholic Church
. . . .
The Roman Catholic Church can teach no . . . .
Through the Roman Catholic Church we receive the seven
. . . . , established by Christ.
What was Christ's promise to the Church?

32. Why Christ Came to Earth

Jesus Christ came to save us from our sins.

Jesus Christ came to show us the way to God.

Jesus Christ came to save us from the effect of Adam's disobedience.

Jesus Christ came to wipe out from our souls original sin.

Jesus Christ came to give grace to our souls.

Christ has told us many ways to secure the grace of God.

He established the Roman Catholic Church as the means to secure this grace of God to men in all ages.

There are seven special ways to secure the grace of God. All of them have an outward sign. These are called Sacraments.

There is a Sacrament to give the soul grace when we become Christians. This is the Sacrament of Baptism. The Sacrament was instituted by Christ.

There is a Sacrament to give the soul grace when we have sinned. This is the Sacrament of Penance. The Sacrament was instituted by Christ.

[84]

There is a Sacrament to give the soul more grace and nourishment after the Sacrament of Penance. This is the Sacrament of Holy Eucharist. The Sacrament was instituted by Christ.

There is a Sacrament to give new strength and grace to the soul. It makes us soldiers of Christ. This is the Sacrament of Confirmation. The Sacrament was instituted by Christ.

There is a Sacrament to give us grace when we are dying. This is the Sacrament of Extreme Unction. The Sacrament was instituted by Christ.

There is a Sacrament to give grace to the souls of people when they are married. This is the Sacrament of Matrimony. The Sacrament was instituted by Christ.

There is a Sacrament to give grace to persons when they are made or ordained priests. This is the Sacrament of Holy Orders. The Sacrament was instituted by Christ.

Each of the seven Sacraments was instituted by Christ.

The Sacraments are ways instituted by Christ to give grace to the soul.

The Sacraments give sanctifying grace to the soul.

We shall study about some of these Sacraments in this book.

We shall study about Baptism, Penance, the Holy Eucharist, and Confirmation.

List five things Christ came to do.
What is a Sacrament?

[85]

What do the Sacraments give to the soul?
How many Sacraments are there?
What Sacrament makes us Christians?
What Sacrament forgives our sins?
What Sacrament gives us nourishment?
What Sacrament makes us soldiers?
What Sacrament gives grace to the dying?
What Sacrament gives grace to people when they are married?
What Sacrament gives grace to a man when ordained priest?
.... instituted the Sacrament of Baptism.
.... instituted the Sacrament of Penance.
.... instituted the Sacrament of Holy Eucharist.
.... instituted the Sacrament of Confirmation.
.... instituted the Sacrament of Extreme Unction.
.... instituted the Sacrament of Matrimony.
.... instituted the Sacrament of Holy Orders.
Christ instituted the .... Sacraments.
The Sacraments give .... grace to the soul.

The Church of Christ

"And I say to thee: That thou art Peter; and upon this rock I will build My church, and the gates of hell shall not prevail against it. * * * And I will give to thee the keys of the kingdom of heaven. And whatsoever thou shalt bind upon earth, it shall be bound also in heaven: and whatsoever thou shalt loose on earth, it shall be loosed also in heaven" (Matt. xvi. 18, 19).

"Going therefore, teach ye all nations; baptizing them in the name of the Father, and of the Son, and of the Holy Ghost. * * * Teaching them to observe all things whatsoever I have commanded you; and behold I am with you all days, even to the consummation of the world" (Matt. xxviii. 19, 20).

33. Christian Doctrine Review
The Church of Christ

48. Which are the means instituted by our Lord to enable men at all times to share in the fruits of the Redemption?
    The means instituted by our Lord to enable men at all times to share in the fruits of the Redemption are the Church and the Sacraments.

49. Who is the invisible Head of the Church?
    Jesus Christ is the invisible Head of the Church.

50. Who is the visible Head of the Church?
    Our Holy Father the Pope, the Bishop of Rome, is the Vicar of Christ on earth and the visible Head of the Church.

51. Why is the Pope, the Bishop of Rome, the visible Head of the Church?
    The Pope, the Bishop of Rome, is the visible Head of the Church because he is the successor of St. Peter, whom Christ made the chief of the Apostles and the visible Head of the Church.

52. Who are the successors of the other Apostles?
    The successors of the other Apostles are the Bishops of the Holy Catholic Church.

53. Why did Christ found the Church?
    Christ founded the Church to teach, govern, sanctify, and save all men.

54. What is the Church?
    The Church is the congregation of all those who profess the faith of Christ, partake of the same Sacraments, and are governed by their lawful pastors under one visible Head.

I baptize thee in the name of the Father, and of the Son,
and of the Holy Ghost.

V. The Sacrament of Baptism

34.   Baptism: Grace in the Soul

The soul comes into the world with original sin. This is the effect of Adam's disobedience on all human souls. The soul lost grace.

But Christ showed the way to restore God's grace to the soul.

This way is called Baptism, which is one of the Sacraments. It is the first Sacrament we receive.

It prepares us for the other Sacraments.

The powers of our souls to understand and to do things are the same.

But the soul is without the grace that is its life.

Baptism gives the soul the grace which is the life of the soul.

It restores the soul to the friendship of God.

It puts the soul on the highway to its home with God.

It is the beginning of the spiritual life of the soul.

Christ told His Apostles to go forth and teach all nations baptizing them in the name of the Father, and of the Son, and of the Holy Ghost.

So we are baptized in the name of the Trinity.

The priest pouring water on the head of the person to be baptized says, "I baptize thee in the name of the Father, and of the Son, and of the Holy Ghost."

In Baptism water is the outward sign or means of
the Sacrament.

What sin was on the baby's soul when it came into this world?
This is the effect of whose disobedience?
Who showed the way to restore God's grace to the soul?
What is this way called?
Which is the first Sacrament we receive?
Baptism prepares for the other ....
Baptism gives .... to the soul.
Baptism makes us .... of God.
Baptism wipes out .... sin.
In Baptism .... is poured on the head of the person
baptized.
While this is done the priest says, I .... thee in the
name of the Father, and of the Son, and of the Holy Ghost.
What is the outward sign in Baptism?

35. The Mark of the Christian

The soul receives grace in Baptism.
It becomes pleasing to God. God loves such a soul.
Baptism leaves in the soul a mark.
It is the mark of the Christian.
It will always remain. It can never be wiped out. No
matter what happens during the life of the man or
woman, it remains. It remains even after death. Even
sin cannot wipe it out. If we commit sin, it makes
our sin worse because, being a Christian, we should
know better.
So Baptism is the beginning of the life of grace of
the soul.

If there was any sin on the soul, it is wiped away by Baptism with original sin. With children, of course, there is no sin in Baptism except original sin.

Baptism fills the soul with the grace of God. The soul becomes very beautiful, indeed. The supernatural life of the soul begins.

In Baptism, the soul receives the mark of the Christian. It is ready to live its life, to start on the highway to God, with Christ's help. The soul is ready to serve under the banner of Christ. The earlier in life this is done, the better for the soul. The soul is also ready and capable of receiving the other Sacraments. The Sacrament of Baptism is the gateway to all the Sacraments. It makes us Christians. It makes possible the entrance of grace into our souls through the other Sacraments.

Baptism gives . . . . to the soul.
Baptism leaves a . . . . in the soul.
It is the mark of a . . . .
This mark can never be . . . .
Baptism makes us . . . .
Baptism wipes away all . . . . from the soul.
Baptism is the gateway to all the . . . .
Baptism starts us on the Highway to . . . .

Baptism

"Going therefore teach ye all nations: baptizing them in the Name of the Father, and of the Son, and of the Holy Ghost" (Matt. xxviii. 19).

"Jesus answered: Amen, amen I say to thee, unless a man be born again of water and the Holy Ghost, he cannot enter into the kingdom of God" (John iii. 5).

36.   Christian Doctrine Review
The Sacrament of Baptism

56. What is a Sacrament?

A Sacrament is an outward sign instituted by Christ to give grace.

57. How many Sacraments are there?

There are seven Sacraments: Baptism, Confirmation, Holy Eucharist, Penance, Extreme Unction, Holy Orders, and Matrimony.

58. Whence have the Sacraments the power of giving grace?

The Sacraments have the power of giving grace from the merits of Jesus Christ.

59. What is Baptism?

Baptism is a Sacrament which cleanses us from original sin, makes us Christians, children of God, and heirs of heaven.

60. How is Baptism given?

Whoever baptizes should pour water on the head of the person to be baptized; and say, while pouring the water: I baptize thee in the name of the Father, and of the Son, and of the Holy Ghost.

VI. The Sacrament of Penance

37. The Soul at Seven Years

The soul comes into the world united to a body.

It does not yet have grace.

It is given grace in Baptism as Christ promised.

It becomes beautiful in the sight of God.

It has the mark of a Christian.

The child lives the happy life of childhood.

The soul remains innocent and beautiful in the sight of God.

It has grace.

The child does not know evil.

He may be naughty to his parents or to other children.

But he does not understand fully about these things.

He grows in body and soul.

He begins to understand more clearly.

He learns as you have just learned about the Commandments of God.

He knows they are Commandments placed on him as on every boy and girl, man and woman.

He knows he must obey them.

He knows that like Adam he will lose God's grace if he *deliberately* disobeys them in *important* matters.

The soul would lose its beauty in the sight of God.

It would lose its grace.

"Father, I have sinned against heaven, and before thee,
I am not now worthy to be called thy son" (Luke xv. 21).

The pure love of God would restore it.

There is danger as we grow older of losing the grace in the soul by not obeying God's Commandments. There is a way to restore it, which Christ showed the Apostles.

He gave them power to restore the grace to the soul by forgiving sin.

He gave the priests of the Catholic Church power to do this in His name.

The soul at the time we are born does not have . . . .
In Baptism the soul receives . . . .
In Baptism the soul receives the . . . . of the Christian.
The soul does not lose the grace of Baptism until it disobeys God's commandments . . . . in an . . . . matter.
Grace can be . . . . to the soul in a way Christ showed the Apostles.
Grace can be restored to the soul by having our . . . . forgiven.
The priests of the Catholic Church in the name of Christ, were given the power to . . . . sin by Christ Himself.

38. Power to Forgive Sins

When we are about seven years old we begin to understand more clearly what the Commandments of God are, and why we should obey them.

But sometimes we are angry and disobey them.

Sometimes we do not think about it and disobey them.

Sometimes we disobey in things that are not of great importance.

In these cases we commit venial sins.

[95]

But we sin greatly if we disobey the Commandments of God, in important matters, when we know what we are doing, and go ahead deliberately and do it. Such a sin is a mortal sin.

Mortal means deathly. A mortal sin is a sin which drives grace out of the soul.

And that is the death of the soul.

When we say the soul is dead we mean there is no grace in the soul.

Man becomes sorry for disobeying God's law.

He wants to return to God. He wants to restore grace in his soul.

Christ showed a way. This shows His great love of man. To restore souls to God was the reason He died on the cross.

Christ died on the cross on Good Friday.

He rose from the dead on Easter Sunday.

He appeared to His Apostles.

He said to them, "Peace be to you."

"As the Father hath sent Me, I also send you."

When He said this He breathed on them, and He said to them — "Receive ye the Holy Ghost."

He then gave them power to forgive sins or to refuse to forgive them.

If they did forgive the sins, God forgave them.

If they refused, the sins were not forgiven.

So the Apostles received the power to forgive sins.

And the priests have the same power today, through God's power.

The outward sign or means of the Sacrament of
Penance is the words of absolution said by the priest.

There are two kinds of sins: .... and ....
If we disobey God in .... matter when we ....
what we are doing, but do it ...., we ....
This sin is a .... sin.
If we disobey God when one of these three things is not true
of our act, the sin is a .... sin.
To be a .... sin we must know what we are doing.
To be a .... sin we must disobey God's law in an
.... matter.
To be a .... sin we must disobey .... one of
God's commandments.
When did Christ give the Apostles the power to ....
sins.
In the Sacrament of .... our sins are forgiven.
Our sins are forgiven by the words of .... said by
the priest.
The words of absolution of the priest is the outward ....
of the Sacrament of Penance.

"Thou art Peter; and upon this rock I will build My church. And I will give to thee the keys of the kingdom of heaven" (Matt. xvi. 18–19).

God's Home

"Mother, where does Jesus dwell?"
Child, He dwelleth everywhere
In the earth and in the air,
In the wide unbending blue —
Even on the farthest star
Where creation's limits are,
Past all ken of me and you!

"Mother, hath He any home?"
First, His home's in heaven bright,
Wondrous mansions built of light,
Then the Tabernacle blest;
But the home He loveth most,
More than Heaven, or Sacred Host,
Is thy sinless, loving breast.
— *E. F. Garesché, S.J.*

39. The Keys of the Kingdom of Heaven

This event after the Resurrection, when Christ gives
the power to forgive sins, goes back to another event
before the Resurrection.

Christ asked His disciples, "Whom do men say that
I am?"

And His disciples told Him, "Some say You are John
the Baptist; and others say that You are a prophet."

Then Christ asked Peter: "Whom do you say I am?"

Peter answered at once from the deep love of Christ
in his heart: "Thou art Christ, the Son of the
Living God."

Then Christ told Peter he would be the first Pope, that He would build His Church on him as on a rock, and nothing could destroy it.

This is the Roman Catholic Church. I believe in the Roman Catholic Church.

And then Christ made to him the promise which was carried out after the Resurrection.

These are Christ's words: Learn them.

"And I will give to thee the keys of the Kingdom of Heaven. And whatsoever thou shalt bind upon earth, it shall be bound also in heaven, and whatsoever thou shalt loose on earth, it shall be loosed in heaven."

Who said the following?

1. "Thou art Christ, the Son of the Living God."
2. "And I will give to thee the keys of the Kingdom of Heaven, and whatsoever thou shalt bind upon earth, it shall be bound also in Heaven, and whatsoever thou shalt loose on earth, it shall be loosed in Heaven."

To whom were the above said?

Who established the Roman Catholic Church?

I believe in the .... Church.

Who was the first Pope?

Who made Peter the head of the Church?

40.   Confession of Sins

How can the sins of him, who has sinned, be forgiven?

A simple way has been provided. This was Christ's plan.

Whenever a soul felt sorry for its sins, and it wanted to return to God and have His grace, the way should be easy. It should always be open where there was true sorrow.

This way is by going to confession.

Before you go into the confessional try to recall whatever mortal sins you have committed.

To help you do this, recall to mind the Ten Commandments and ask yourself the questions under each that are given in this book. Other questions might help you too. This is called examination of conscience.

We go to the priest in the confessional.

We kneel down.

He can hear your voice but he cannot see your face.

You ask his blessing. "Bless me Father. I have sinned."

He blesses you.

You say the first time. "This is my first confession."

You then tell him whatever mortal sins that come to your mind that you have committed.

If you do not remember having committed a mortal sin, tell him some venial sin.

You must remember that you cannot be forgiven your sins unless you are sorry that you sinned. The priest asks you to say an Act of Contrition or sorrow.

Your teacher will teach you an Act of Contrition.

Bless me Father, I have sinned.

I absolve thee in the name of the Father, and of the Son,
and of the Holy Ghost.

While you are saying your Act of Contrition the priest forgives you your sins.

He does this "in the name of the Father, and of the Son, and of the Holy Ghost."

He gives you some prayers to say. These prayers are called the penance.

After your first confession you will not say, "This is my first confession."

You tell the priest two things.

How long it was since your last confession.

You say, "I have been away from confession one week, or two weeks."

Did you say your penance?

You say, "I said my penance."

If we read over now what is required to receive the Sacrament of Penance worthily, we will find that there are five things.

These five things are:

1. To recall to mind any sins we may have committed by an examination of conscience
2. To feel a real sorrow for our sins.
3. To make up our minds that we shall make every effort to sin no more.
4. To confess our sins to a priest.
5. To carry out or fulfill the penance which the priest has given us.

Now we shall learn about Holy Communion.

The sinner who is truly .... for his sins may have them forgiven.

The way to forgiveness is always . . . .
This simple and easy way is to go to . . . .
What are the five things necessary for a worthy confession?
What is the confessional?
What is the examination of conscience?
What is contrition? What is penance?

Penance

"If thou wilt enter into life, keep the Commandments" (Matt. xix. 17).

"If you will not forgive men, neither will your Father forgive you your offenses" (Matt. vi. 15).

"All the law is fulfilled in one word: Thou shalt love thy neighbor as thyself" (Gal. v. 14).

"Master, which is the great commandment in the law? Jesus said to him: Thou shalt love the Lord thy God with thy whole heart, and with thy whole soul, and with thy whole mind. This is the greatest and the first commandment. And the second is like to this: Thou shalt love thy neighbor, as thyself. On these two commandments dependeth the whole law and the prophets" (Matt. xxii. 36–40).

"I will give to thee the Keys of the Kingdom of Heaven. And whatsoever thou shalt bind upon earth, shall be bound also in Heaven: and whatsoever thou shalt loose on earth, shall be loosed also in Heaven" (Matt. xvi. 19).

41. Christian Doctrine Review
The Sacrament of Penance

62. What is a Sacrament?

A Sacrament is an outward sign instituted by Christ to give grace.

63. How many Sacraments are there?

There are seven Sacraments: Baptism, Confirmation, Holy Eucharist, Penance, Extreme Unction, Holy Orders, and Matrimony.

64. Whence have the Sacraments the power of giving grace?

The Sacraments have the power of giving grace from the merits of Jesus Christ.

65. What is the Sacrament of Penance?

Penance is a Sacrament in which the sins committed after Baptism are forgiven.

66. What must we do to receive the Sacrament of Penance worthily?

To receive the Sacrament of Penance worthily we must do five things:

1. We must examine our conscience.
2. We must have sorrow for our sins.
3. We must make a firm resolution never more to offend God.
4. We must confess our sins to the priest.
5. We must accept the penance which the priest gives us.

VII. The Sacrament of the Holy Eucharist

42. The Holy Eucharist

The soul after confession is happy.

The grace of God is restored to it.

It is beautiful in the sight of God.

It is possible for the soul to be happy and to have more grace.

Grace, we know, is the life of the soul.

Christ told us that unless we eat of His Body and Blood, we shall not have life.

The soul must have food and drink to keep its life as the body does.

What is this food and drink of the soul?

It is the Body and Blood of Christ.

We have learned that Christ gave the priests of the Catholic Church the power to change bread and wine into the Body and Blood of Christ.

We have learned that this power to change the bread and the wine into the Body and Blood of Christ is used by the priest in the Mass.

The species of bread and wine are the outward signs of the Sacrament of the Holy Eucharist.

Grace is the .... of the soul.

What is the food of the soul?

What power have priests of the Roman Catholic Church?

When do they exercise this power?

"As often as ye do these things, ye shall do them in remembrance of Me" (*Missal*).

What is the outward sign of the Sacrament of the Holy
Eucharist?

A Child's Wish

I wish I were the little key
  That locks Love's Captive in,
And lets Him out to go and free
  A sinful heart from sin.

I wish I were the little bell
  That tinkles for the Host,
When God comes down each day to dwell
  With hearts He loves the most.

I wish I were the chalice fair,
  That holds the Blood of Love,
When every flash lights holy prayer
  Upon its way above.

I wish I were the little flower
  So near the Host's sweet face,
Or like the light that half an hour
  Burned on the shrine of grace.

I wish I were the altar where,
  As on His Mother's breast,
Christ nestles, like a child, fore'er
  In Eucharistic rest.

But, Oh! my God, I wish the most
  That my poor heart may be
A home all holy for each Host
  That comes in love to me.

                    — *Father Ryan*

May the Body of our Lord Jesus Christ preserve thy
soul to life everlasting. Amen.

43. Holy Communion

In the Mass the bread and wine become the Body and Blood of Christ.

When the priest says, "This is My Body," the bread is no longer ordinary bread, it is the Body of Christ.

When the priest says, "This is My Blood," the wine is no longer ordinary wine, it is the Blood of Christ.

The priest receives in his Communion the Body and Blood of Christ under the form of bread and wine.

This is the food and drink of the soul.

You may receive it, too.

It is given to you and to me in the form of the Host.

The Host is the Body and Blood of Christ, too.

It is the food of our soul.

We should receive It often, as often as possible.

However, we can receive It but once a day.

We should receive the Body and Blood in Holy Communion weekly, or at least monthly.

We must be in a state of grace before we go to Holy Communion.

We go to confession on Saturday afternoon or evening and receive Communion on Sunday at Mass.

We may receive Communion on holydays and on week days.

We may receive Communion as often as we are in a state of grace, without going to confession for every Communion.

We should go to confession and to Holy Communion often.

We must go to Holy Communion at least once a year at Easter time.

Some people, young and old, go to Holy Communion every day.

We know that to go to Communion we must be in a state of grace. This we secure ordinarily by going to confession.

We must do something else. From midnight to the time we go to Mass to receive Communion we must not eat nor drink.

We wait for Mass. We follow the priest closely. We prepare ourselves for this great gift. It is time to go to the altar to receive Holy Communion. We go slowly and reverently.

We receive the Body and Blood of Christ.

How happy that makes us.

I give thanks to God for His Son's love and sacrifice for me.

God loves me and I love God.

Christ loves me and I love Christ.

The Holy Ghost loves me and I love the Holy Ghost.

I hope this food, which is the Body and Blood of Christ, will save my soul to eternal life.

I am sure it will.

How good God is.

I love God.

In Holy Communion we receive the . . . . and . . . . of Christ.

In the Mass, the bread and wine are changed into the . . . . and . . . . of Christ.

We must be in a state of grace to receive . . . .

We must have . . . . from midnight to receive Holy Communion.

What two conditions are necessary to receive Holy Communion?

Which of the following practices will you try to follow?

1. We may go to Holy Communion once a day.
2. We should go to Communion weekly, or at least monthly.
3. We must go to Communion once a year, at Eastertime, to be a practical Catholic.

After Communion

Dear God, dear God, You came to me!
How glad I am! And yet I see
I am not what I ought to be
Here is my heart; It's small, but I
Have filled it up with love. I'll try
To keep it that way till I die.
— *Mary Dixon Thayer*

44. Christ Speaks to the Soul

Christ speaks to the soul.

Long ago I told men that their souls would have no life or grace, unless they ate My Body and Blood.

For My Flesh is meat indeed, and My Blood is drink indeed.

I multiply this food and drink of the soul by the same power that I multiplied the fishes and the loaves to feed the many people who listened to Me in the mountain.

I died on the cross that you might have this food for your soul.

I am the Living Bread Which came down from Heaven.

I am the Good Shepherd Who love My sheep. I gave My life for My sheep. You are My sheep.

I love you with an everlasting love.

I love you as God loves His children. As the Father hath loved Me, I also have loved you.

I love to be in your soul.

I give it peace. My peace I give to your soul.

Let not your heart be troubled nor let it be afraid.

Love God, love your enemies. Do good to them that hate you. Pray for them, too.

Come to Me always and I will refresh you, for I am the Way, the Truth, and the Life.

Write a number of sentences that you would think Christ might say to your soul.

45. The Soul Speaks to Christ

The Soul speaks to Christ.

Of so great a gift as God Himself, I am not worthy.

What have I done to deserve so much from God?

Lord, I am not worthy that Thou shouldst enter into my soul. Please say only the word, and my soul shall be healed.

I have sinned but I am truly sorry for all my sins.

I love You.

I love You, because You are the Good Shepherd.

I wish to know You better.

I wish to love You with all my soul.

I wish to serve You, and for You, my neighbor.

I go to Holy Communion because it is Your will.

Thy will be done, not mine.

What peace comes to my soul in Holy Communion!

What joy! What happiness!

I give Thee thanks.

I give praise to Thee, Lord, with my whole heart.

I praise Thy holy Name.

I love Thee. I shall keep Thy Commandments.

Take me to Thy breast on the last day.

Write a number of sentences which tell how your soul feels toward Christ, particularly after Holy Communion.

Thy Little One

Dear Lord, let me recount to Thee
Some of the great things Thou hast done
    For me, even me
    Thy little one.

It was not I that car'd for Thee —
But Thou didst set Thy heart upon
    Me, even me
    Thy little one.

And therefore was it sweet to Thee
To leave Thy Majesty and Throne,
    And grow like me
    A Little One

A swaddled Baby on the knee
Of a dear Mother of Thine own,
    Quite weak like me
    Thy little one.

Jerusalem and Galilee —
Thy love embrace not those alone
    But also me
    Thy little one.

Thy unblemished Body on the Tree
Was bar'd and broken to atone
    For me, for me
    Thy little one.

Thou lovest me upon the Tree —
Still me, hid by the ponderous stone —
Me always — me
Thy little one.

And love of me arose with Thee
When death and hell lay overthrown
Thou lovest me
Thy little one.

And love of me went up with Thee
To sit upon Thy Father's Throne:
Thou lovest me
Thy little one.

Lord, as Thou me, so would I Thee
Love in pure love's communion,
For Thou lov'st me
Thy little one.

Which love of me bring back with Thee
To judgment when the Trump is blown,
Still loving me
Thy little one.
— *Christina G. Rossetti*

Heaven

Oh, heaven I think must be always
Quite like a First Communion day,
With love so sweet and joy so strange;
For heaven above will never change.
— *Father Faber*

Eucharist

"Thomas answered, and said to Him: 'My Lord, and my God' " (John xx. 28).

"This is the Bread which cometh down from heaven; that if any man eat of it, he may not die" (John vi. 50).

"And taking bread, He gave thanks, and brake: and gave to them, saying: 'This is My body, which is given for you. Do this for a commemoration of Me' " (Luke xxii. 19).

"If any man eat of this Bread, he shall live for ever; and the Bread that I will give, is My flesh, for the life of the world" (John vi. 52).

"Whilst they were at Supper, Jesus took bread, and blessed and broke: and gave to His Disciples, and said: Take ye, and eat: This is My Body. And taking the Chalice He gave thanks: and gave to them, saying: Drink ye all of this. For This is My Blood of the New Testament which shall be shed for many unto remission of sins" (Matt. xxvi. 26–28).

"Labor not for the meat which perisheth, but for that which endureth unto life everlasting, which the Son of Man will give you. For Him hath God, the Father, sealed" (John vi. 27).

"Lord, I am not worthy that Thou shouldst enter under my roof: but only say the word, and my soul shall be healed" (Matt. viii. 8). (From the Mass. This passage is based on Matt. viii. 8. Where the Centurion says to Christ: "Lord I am not worthy that Thou shouldst enter under my roof: but only say the word, and my *servant* shall be healed.")

46.   Christian Doctrine Review

The Sacrament of the Holy Eucharist

68. What is a Sacrament?
A Sacrament is an outward sign instituted by Christ to give grace.

69. How many Sacraments are there?
There are seven Sacraments: Baptism, Confirmation, Holy Eucharist, Penance, Extreme Unction, Holy Orders and Matrimony.

70. Whence have the Sacraments the power of giving grace?
The Sacraments have the power of giving grace from the merits of Jesus Christ.

71. What is the Holy Eucharist?
The Holy Eucharist is the Sacrament which contains the Body and Blood, Soul and Divinity, of our Lord Jesus Christ under the appearances of bread and wine.

72. When did Christ institute the Holy Eucharist?
Christ instituted the Holy Eucharist at the Last Supper, the night before He died.

73. Who were present when our Lord instituted the Holy Eucharist?
When our Lord instituted the Holy Eucharist the twelve Apostles were present.

74. How are we united to Jesus Christ in the Holy Eucharist?
We are united to Jesus Christ in the Holy Eucharist by means of Holy Communion.

75. What is Holy Communion?
Holy Communion is the receiving of the Body and Blood of Christ.

76. What is necessary to make a good Communion?
   To make a good Communion it is necessary to be in the state of sanctifying grace and to be fasting from midnight.
77. Is it well to receive Holy Communion often?
   It is well to receive Holy Communion often, as nothing is a greater aid to a holy life than often to receive the Author of all grace and the Source of all good.
78. When and where are the bread and wine changed into the Body and Blood of Christ?
   The bread and wine are changed into the Body and Blood of Christ at the Consecration in the Mass.
79. What is the Mass?
   The Mass is the unbloody sacrifice of the Body and Blood of Christ.
80. Is the Mass the same sacrifice as that of the cross?
   The Mass is the same sacrifice as that of the cross.

The Very Time

I used to think, if I'd been bad,
I'd better stay away
From You, dear God, I used to think
I might as well not pray.
I used to think, if I'd been bad,
You wouldn't want me to —
And so I didn't pray, but now
Of course I always do.
Now when I have been bad, dear God,
I always quickly fall
Down on my knees for then — Oh! then
I need You most of all!
                          — *Mary Dixon Thayer*

VIII. The Sacrament of Confirmation

47. Before Confirmation

The soul of man begins its life as a Christian with Baptism.

It then receives the grace of God.

It loses original sin.

It keeps the grace of God ordinarily for about seven years, and may to the end of its life.

About this time the child begins to understand what sin is. He becomes responsible for his actions.

Sin is disobedience to God's Commandments.

We learn God's Commandments in order that we may keep them.

We keep them to show our love of God.

But if we are so weak as to disobey God's Commandments, in an important matter, and we do it deliberately, we commit mortal sins.

We lose the grace of God.

We need forgiveness for our sins.

We go to confession.

God forgives us our sins.

Grace is restored to our soul.

We are ready for the food of the soul.

We receive the Holy Eucharist.

Christ is in the soul.

There is more grace, more life.

The soul is beautiful in the sight of God.

We go frequently to the altar to receive this food of the soul.

We gain strength, we gain grace, we become more like God.

There is another step in the growth of the soul.

Let us see what it is.

When do we begin life as Christians?

What Sacrament starts us on the King's Highway as a child of God?

What precious gift is given to us in Baptism?

What do we call the guideposts and rules along the King's Highway?

When we keep the Commandments what do we show to God?

When we disobey the Commandments what happens to our soul?

After we have lost grace by mortal sin how do we find it again?

What Sacrament restores grace to our soul after we have lost it by disobeying the Commandments?

What is the Sacrament that is food for our souls?

How does the Holy Eucharist make our souls in the sight of God?

How are we helped if we receive the Holy Eucharist often?

48. The Soldiers of Christ

Christ provided another means or Sacrament to give the soul more grace and the special grace to be a soldier of Christ.

We have the food to nourish the soul in Holy Communion.

We meet in life many temptations.

We meet difficulties.

As we grow older, it is more difficult for us.

We need more strength.

We need more grace.

We must be ready to show our faith in God.

We must become more active in our efforts to gain eternal life.

Christ established the Sacrament of Confirmation.

We are prepared for it by learning things such as are given in this book about God, the Father, Jesus, the Son of God, and the Holy Ghost, the Blessed Trinity.

The priest tells us if we are ready to be confirmed.

Only the bishop or archbishop can confirm.

He comes to the parish church.

All to be confirmed go to Holy Communion in the morning.

The bishop confirms a person who has received Baptism by signing his forehead with oil or chrism.

When he does this, he says, "I sign thee with the Sign of the Cross, and I confirm thee with the chrism of salvation; in the name of the Father, and of the Son, and of the Holy Ghost. Amen."

The bishop then strikes each person confirmed a gentle blow on the cheek. This is to remind each person that he may expect blows for Christ. He must have strength and grace to take these blows. He must be a soldier.

I sign thee with the Sign of the Cross, and I confirm thee with the chrism of salvation; in the name of the Father, and of the Son, and of the Holy Ghost. Amen.

Peace be with you.

Find as many reasons as you can why Christ instituted the
Sacrament of Confirmation.

How are we prepared for Confirmation?

Who can confirm?

What does the bishop do in Confirmation?

What does the bishop say in confirming a person?

Why does the bishop give each person confirmed a gentle blow
on the cheek?

49.   The Holy Ghost

The Holy Ghost is the Third Person of the Blessed
Trinity.

The Holy Ghost is God.

I believe in the Holy Ghost.

In Confirmation the soul receives the graces and gifts
of the Holy Ghost.

These graces and gifts of the Holy Ghost are a great
source of strength to the soul.

They give us the strength of soldiers.

We are armed for the battle of life.

We are ready to tell our faith in God.

We are ready to tell and to show our love of God, and
of all God's creatures.

The Holy Ghost is the .... Person of the Blessed
Trinity.

The Holy Ghost is ....

We receive in Confirmation the .... and .... of
the Holy Ghost.

The graces and gifts of the Holy Ghost make us ....
as soldiers.

[126]

The graces and gifts of the Holy Ghost prepare us for the
.... of life.
The graces and gifts of the Holy Ghost make us ready to
tell our .... in God.
The graces and gifts of the Holy Ghost make us ready to
show our .... for God.

50.   The Mark of the Soldier of Christ

Baptism leaves in the soul the mark of the Christian.

It cannot be taken away from the soul. It is there
forever.

The Sacrament of Baptism can be received only once.

Confirmation is like Baptism.

Confirmation leaves a mark in the soul. It is the mark
of the soldier of Christ. It cannot be taken away
from the soul. It is there forever.

The Sacrament of Confirmation can be received only
once.

We can, however, go to confession and receive the Holy
Eucharist as often and as frequently as we desire it.
But, however, we can receive Holy Communion only
once a day.

Confirmation, like Baptism, leaves on the soul a ....

This mark cannot be ....

This mark lasts ....

Two of the Sacraments that leave a mark on the soul are
.... and ....

Confirmation like Baptism can be received only ....

Two Sacraments that can be received only once are ....
and ....

Holy Communion can be received ....

[127]

"Then they laid their hands upon them, and they received the Holy Ghost" (Acts viii. 17).

"I will ask the Father, and He shall give you another Paraclete, that He may abide with you for ever" (John xiv. 16).

51. Christian Doctrine Review
The Sacrament of Confirmation

82. What is a Sacrament?
A Sacrament is an outward sign instituted by Christ to give grace.

83. How many Sacraments are there?
There are seven Sacraments: Baptism, Confirmation, Holy Eucharist, Penance, Extreme Unction, Holy Orders, and Matrimony.

84. Whence have the Sacraments the power of giving grace?
The Sacraments have the power of giving grace from the merits of Jesus Christ.

85. What is Confirmation?
Confirmation is a Sacrament through which we receive the Holy Ghost to make us strong and perfect Christians and soldiers of Jesus Christ.

86. Who administers Confirmation?
The bishop is the ordinary minister of Confirmation.

87. How does the bishop give Confirmation?
The bishop extends his hands over those who are to be confirmed, prays that they may receive the Holy

Ghost, and anoints the forehead of each with holy chrism in the form of a cross.

88. What does the bishop say in anointing the person he confirms?

In anointing the person he confirms the bishop says: I sign thee with the Sign of the Cross, and I confirm thee with the chrism of salvation, in the name of the Father, and of the Son, and of the Holy Ghost. Amen.

89. Why does the bishop give the person he confirms a slight blow on the cheek?

The bishop gives the person he confirms a slight blow on the cheek, to put him in mind that he must be ready to suffer everything, even death, for the sake of Christ.

IX. Conclusion

52. I Go to Prepare a Place for You

The desire of God for the human soul is very great, indeed.

The coming of Christ showed this great love of God.

The death of Christ on the cross showed Christ's great love of men and women, His great love of boys and girls.

The way Christ showed us that we might keep close to Him, is a simple way. It is always open.

We see Him at the entrance to it saying, "Come to Me, all ye who are heavily burdened and I will refresh you."

Do you love God as He loves you?

Do you seek Him as He seeks you?

Do you go to Him in Holy Communion often?

Do you go to Him every week?

Remember Christ died for you.

He ascended into Heaven.

He said, "In My Father's house there are many mansions. If it were not so I would have told you. I go to prepare a place for you."

He added: "And if I shall go and prepare a place for you, I will come again and will take you to Myself, for where I am, you also may be."

List the proofs of Christ's love for us that you can give.

Now make a list of ways in which you can prove your love for Christ.

What do Christ's words mean: "Come to Me all ye who are heavily burdened and I will refresh you"?

What place has Christ prepared for you?

What did Christ mean by "In My Father's house"?

What do you think Heaven is?

What words of Christ about our soul should we always keep in mind?

The End of Man

"In My Father's house there are many mansions. If not, I would have told you: because I go to prepare a place for you" (John xiv. 2).

"And if I shall go, and prepare a place for you, I will come again, and will take you to Myself: that where I am, you also may be" (John xiv. 3).

"This day thou shalt be with Me in Paradise" (Luke xxiii. 43).

"Not every one that saith to Me, Lord, Lord, shall enter into the Kingdom of Heaven; but he that doth the will of My Father Who is in Heaven, he shall enter into the Kingdom of Heaven" (Matt. vii. 21).

53. Christian Doctrine Review
Conclusion

91. How does God punish those who do not keep His Commandments?

    God punishes in Hell those who do not keep His Commandments.

92. What did Jesus Christ suffer?

    Jesus Christ suffered a bloody sweat, a cruel scourging, was crowned with thorns, and was crucified.

93. On what day did Christ die?

    Christ died on Good Friday.

94. Why do you call that day "good" on which Christ died so sorrowful a death?

    We call the day good on which Christ died, because by His death He showed His great love for man, and purchased for him every blessing.

95. Where did Christ die?

    Christ died on Mount Calvary.

96. How did Christ die?

    Christ was nailed to the cross and died on it between two thieves.

97. Why did Christ suffer and die?

    Christ suffered and died for our sins.

98. What words should we bear always in mind?

    We should bear always in mind these words of our Lord and Savior Jesus Christ: "What doth it profit a man if he gain the whole world and suffer the loss of his own soul, or what exchange shall a man give for his soul? For the Son of Man shall come in the glory of His Father with His angels; and then will He render to every man according to his works."

I believe in God the Father Almighty, Creator of heaven and earth; and in Jesus Christ his only Son, our Lord; Who was conceived by the Holy Ghost, born of the Virgin Mary, suffered under Pontius Pilate, was crucified, died, and was buried. He descended into hell; the third day He arose again from the dead: He ascended into heaven, sitteth at the right hand of God, the Father Almighty: from thence He shall come to judge the living and the dead.

I believe in the Holy Ghost, the holy Catholic Church, the communion of saints, the forgiveness of sins, the resurrection of the body, and life everlasting. Amen.

W.B.H.

54. The Apostles' Creed

I believe in God, the Father Almighty, Creator of
Heaven and earth,
And in Jesus Christ, His only Son, our Lord,
Who was conceived by the Holy Ghost,
Born of the Virgin Mary,
Suffered under Pontius Pilate,
Was crucified, died, and was buried.
He descended into Hell,
The third day He arose again from the dead,
He ascended into Heaven,
Sitteth at the right hand of God, the Father Almighty,
From thence He shall come to judge the living and
the dead.
I believe in the Holy Ghost,
The Holy Catholic Church,
The Communion of Saints,
The forgiveness of sins,
The resurrection of the body,
And life everlasting.
Amen.

I believe in God the ....
I believe in God the ....
I believe in God the ....
I believe in the .... Church.
I believe in the .... of Saints.
I believe in the forgiveness of ....
I believe in the .... of the body.
I believe in .... everlasting.

55.   Prayers

The Sign of the Cross

In the name of the Father, and of the Son, and of the Holy Ghost. Amen.

The Lord's Prayer, or Our Father

Our Father, who art in heaven, hallowed be Thy name; Thy kingdom come; Thy will be done on earth as it is in heaven. Give us this day our daily bread; and forgive us our trespasses as we forgive those who trespass against us; and lead us not into temptation; but deliver us from evil. Amen.

The Angelical Salutation, or Hail Mary

Hail Mary, full of grace, the Lord is with thee. Blessed art thou among women, and blessed is the fruit of thy womb, Jesus. Holy Mary, Mother of God, pray for us sinners, now and at the hour of our death. Amen.

The Apostles' Creed, or I Believe in God

I believe in God the Father Almighty, Creator of heaven and earth; and in Jesus Christ, His only Son, our Lord, who was conceived of the Holy Ghost, born of the Virgin Mary, suffered under Pontius Pilate, was crucified; died and was buried; He descended into hell;

the third day He rose again from the dead; He ascended into heaven, sitteth at the right hand of God, the Father Almighty; from thence He shall come to judge the living and the dead. I believe in the Holy Ghost; the Holy Catholic Church; the communion of saints; the forgiveness of sins; the resurrection of the body; and life everlasting. Amen.

The Confiteor, or I Confess

I confess to Almighty God, to blessed Mary ever Virgin, to blessed Michael the Archangel, to blessed John the Baptist, to the holy Apostles Peter and Paul, and to all the saints, that I have sinned exceedingly in thought, word, and deed, *through my fault, through my fault, through my most grievous fault.* Therefore, I beseech blessed Mary ever Virgin, blessed Michael the Archangel, blessed John the Baptist, the holy Apostles Peter and Paul, and all the saints, to pray to the Lord our God for me.

May the Almighty God have mercy on me, forgive me my sins, and bring me to everlasting life. Amen.

May the Almighty and Merciful Lord grant me pardon, absolution, and remission of all my sins. Amen.

The Gloria Patri, or the Lesser Doxology

Glory be to the Father, and to the Son, and to the Holy Ghost. As it was in the beginning, is now, and ever shall be, world without end. Amen.

Acts of the Three Divine or Theological Virtues

1. An Act of Faith

O my God! I firmly believe that Thou art one God in three Divine Persons, Father, Son, and Holy Ghost. I believe that the Divine Son became man, and died for our sins, and that He will come to judge the living and the dead. I believe these and all the truths which the Holy Catholic Church teaches, because Thou hast revealed them, who canst neither deceive nor be deceived.

2. An Act of Hope

O my God! relying on Thy infinite goodness and promises, I hope to obtain pardon of my sins, the help of Thy grace, and life everlasting, through the merits of Jesus Christ, my Lord and Redeemer.

3. An Act of Charity, or Love

O my God! I love Thee above all things, with my whole heart and soul, because Thou art all-good and worthy of all love. I love my neighbor as myself, for love of Thee. I forgive all who have injured me, and ask pardon of all whom I have injured.

An Act of Contrition

O my God! I am heartily sorry for having offended Thee, and I detest all my sins, because I dread the loss of heaven and the pains of hell, but most of all because they offend Thee, my God, who art all-good and deserving of all my love. I firmly resolve, with the help of Thy grace, to confess my sins, to do penance, and to amend my life.

Blessing Before Meals

Bless us, O Lord, and these Thy gifts, which we are about to receive from Thy bounty, through Christ our Lord. Amen.

Thanksgiving After Meals

We return Thee thanks, Almighty God, for these Thy benefits, which we have received from Thy bounty, through Christ, our Lord. Amen.

The Angelus

(At morning, noon, and night)

V. The angel of the Lord declared unto Mary.
R. And she conceived of the Holy Ghost.
   Hail Mary, etc.
V. Behold the handmaid of the Lord.
R. Be it done unto me according to Thy word.
   Hail Mary, etc.
V. And the Word was made flesh.

R. And dwelt among us.

Hail Mary, etc.

V. Pray for us, O holy Mother of God.

R. That we may be made worthy of the promises of Christ.

Lay Baptism

The Manner in Which a Lay Person Is to Baptize in Case of Necessity

Pour common water on the head of the person to be baptized, and say while pouring it:

"I baptize thee in the name of the Father, and of the Son, and of the Holy Ghost."

Prayers After Communion

Pour forth, we beseech Thee, O Lord, Thy grace into our hearts, that we, to whom the Incarnation of Christ Thy Son was made known by the message of an Angel, may, by His Passion and Cross, be brought to the glory of His Resurrection.

———

We humbly beseech Thee, O God Almighty, that Thou wouldst grant to those whom Thou refreshest with Thy Sacraments that they may serve Thee worthily by a life pleasing to Thee.

———

May this Communion, O Lord, cleanse us from sin: and by the intercession of Blessed Mary, the Virgin Mother of God, unite us in Him Who is the heavenly healer of souls.

May the Sacrament we have received, O Lord, take from us all craving for the sinful delights of earth, and nourish our souls to life eternal, through Christ, our Lord.

———

Thou hast feasted us, O Lord, at Thy banquet of heavenly delights; may we ever hunger after that which truly nourishes us, through Christ, our Lord.

———

We humbly beseech Thee, Almighty God, that, refreshed by Thy Most Holy Sacrament, we may henceforth, by holiness of life, ever render an acceptable service to Thee, through Christ, our Lord.

———

We beseech Thee, O Lord, that the Sacrament we have received may both be food to our souls and sure protection to our bodies, through Christ, our Lord.

———

Abide with us always, O Lord, our God, so that, by the Sacrament we have received, we may be cleansed from all sin and delivered from all dangers, through Christ, our Lord.

———

Filled, O Lord, with Thy heavenly gifts: may we by Thy grace ever remain in thanksgiving for the same, through Christ, our Lord.

———

Thou hast filled us with heavenly food, O Lord: grant, we beseech Thee, that we may be cleansed from our hidden faults, and delivered from the snares of our enemies, through Christ, our Lord.

―――――

May Thy sacraments, O Lord, at all times purify and strengthen us: and may they lead us to eternal salvation, through Christ, our Lord.

―――――

In order, O Lord, that we may be worthy to receive Thy Adorable Sacrament, make us, we beseech Thee at all times observant of Thy commandments, through Christ, our Lord.

―――――

Fed with the Bread of immortal life, O Lord: we beseech Thee, that what has passed our lips may be food for our souls, through Christ, our Lord.

Brief Prayers and Aspirations

Jesus, my God, I love Thee above all things.

My Lord and my God.

O sweet Heart of Jesus, I implore, that I may ever love Thee more and more.

Lord, have mercy on us (3),

Christ, have mercy on us (3),

Lord, have mercy on us (3).

Lord, save us, we perish.

Who the day before He suffered took bread into His holy and venerable hands, and with His eyes lifted up towards heaven, to God, His almighty Father, giving thanks to Thee, did bless, break, and give to His disciples, saying: Take, and eat ye all of this; for This is My Body.

Jesus, meek and humble of heart, make my heart like unto Thine.

Jesus, I adore Thee.

Jesus, Mary, and Joseph, I love Thee.

Blessed be Jesus Christ, true God and true Man.

Blessed be the great Mother of God, Mary most holy.

In like manner, after He had supped, taking also this excellent chalice into His holy and venerable hands, and giving Thee thanks, He blest, and gave to His disciples, saying:

Take, and drink ye all of this; for this is the chalice of My Blood of the new and eternal testament; the mystery of faith; which shall be shed for you, and for many, to the remission of sins. As often as ye do these things, ye shall do them in remembrance of Me....

Let us give thanks to the Lord, our God

Lord, Thou knowest that I love Thee.

Lord, teach me to pray.

Jesus, Mary, Joseph.

Jesus, Mary, Joseph, I give You my heart and soul.

Hallowed be Thy name.

Infant Jesus, bless us.

Blessed be God.

Eternal rest give unto them, O Lord, and let perpetual light shine upon them.

Sweet Heart of Jesus, be my love.

Sacred Heart of Jesus, I trust in Thee.

Lamb of God Who takest away the sins of the world, have mercy on us.

My Lord and my God.

May the Body and Blood of our Lord Jesus Christ preserve my soul to everlasting life.

My Jesus, mercy!

Let us give thanks to the Lord, our God.

May the Almighty and merciful Lord grant us pardon, absolution, and remission of our sins.

Jesus, in the Most Holy Sacrament, have mercy on us.